THREE VILLAGES

An Autobiography

by

DONAL FOLEY

BALLYLOUGH BOOKS

First Published 1977 by the Egotist Press
33, Rialto Cottages, Dublin 8.
This edition published 2003 by Ballylough Books
Callaghane, Co. Waterford, Ireland.
Phone: 051 – 382538
e-mail : info@fewerconsulting.com

ISBN 09533704-3-7

Cover design by Rachel Foley

Printed in the Republic of Ireland
by
Modern Printers, Kilkenny.

INTRODUCTION BY MAEVE BINCHY

For the friends of Donal Foley, and we are many, he never really died at all. He just went away for a bit.

I cannot count the number of times over the years when I have noted things I wanted to tell him, even going so far as to cut something out of a newspaper that I knew would interest him.

For us and for all who read and enjoyed his columns it will be a joy to see Three Villages once more in print. The stories old and new are set in three backdrops; the Waterford village of Ferrybank and two capital cities, London and Dublin, all tamed and defined by a man whose powers of observation and enthusiasm could have made anywhere his home.

One of Donal's great strengths is that he can recall and be absorbed by his past, by the culture that was De Valera's Ireland, and yet not become a prisoner of it. Never do you hear him whining and wishing that things had not changed or had changed more. Emigration was a fact, poverty was a condition. Hope was plentiful, disappointment was everywhere, families and friendships were unbreakable.

People sent money home as a matter of course. No one's expectations were too high.

When Donal's father went to Dublin on a winter's morning in 1936 to see the specialist who confirmed his cancer, he wore an overcoat given to him by the parish priest. When Donal began work as a young postman he was stunned by the generous cups of tea at almost every halt and the big cooked breakfast in the monastery.

He watched the midwife's stylish court shoes and shapely black stockinged legs as she visited their home regularly every two years to add a new baby to the family, and there were the magnificent family holidays in Ring where fourteen of the Foleys would get into 'The Linnet', the open lorry hired from Ring Co-op, and make the journey via Dungarvan for their holiday in the Gaeltacht.

It was all new and exciting, not only the different language spoken, but the invitation to eat mackerel and boiled potatoes in every cottage and the advice from his mother to praise the potatoes of the house unstintingly as that was the best compliment you could pay.

He goes to London and works in various jobs from railway stations onwards towards the journalism that was to be what made him famous.

He met and married Pat Dowling and together they went to ceilis in Clapham Common where he remembers an Irish recitation during the Blitz….. "May God's curse be on you England." Donal remarks mildly that as the bombs were falling outside the ceili hall the Creator seemed already to be doing his anti-British bit that night, a point lost on the recitor of the poem.

He is always non-judgemental, finding much to praise in the working-class solidarity of the English, the infectious joy and relief of the cockneys at the end of the War, the street scenes when Londoners, hearing their Irish accents, urged them to sing *When Irish Eyes Are Smiling* in the middle of *Knees Up Mother Brown* and *The Old Kent Road.*

And then, years later, he came back to his third village which was Dublin.

And that's where I met him and knew him and he changed my life by giving me a chance to write in *The Irish Times* when others might have said that a 27 year-old teacher without a day's experience of newspaper work was not the wisest choice.

He was a friend, an advisor, a teacher and a delight.

We would have done anything to please him and make him proud of us—the people he spotted and in whom he placed his whole faith and his reputation.

And even though I have never believed that he really died I will always remember with great delight and warmth his last words to his dear wife Pat.

She was reassuring him that even though he might lose his speech he would be able to hear and respond, pressing once for 'yes' and twice for 'no'.

Donal thought for a moment and asked what was the point of speaking if you could only say yes or no. For the wonderful observer of human life and great communicator that he was, this was an unanswerable question.

No point at all Donal, let your thoughts and memories and views live on for ever.

Maeve Binchy 2003

INTRODUCTION BY MARY MAHER

July, 2003 – A senior appointment in Irish media has just been announced. As usual, the punters in the pubs are avidly debating the merits of the successful candidate compared to those he defeated. No question but that the right choice was made, says one long-time observer of the scene; whatever his failings, the victor had the crucial and elusive edge.

"Something of a Donal Foley there, you know?" he added.

We knew. It is some summation of the man that twenty-two years after his death he is still the standard for those who remember him, and that his tenure in *The Irish Times* is the legend we press on new generations of journalists. We knew that what had just been identified—the "something" about Donal Foley—was a combination of qualities, often unorthodox, paradoxical, and very rare indeed.

First of all, anyone with that "something" would have a sense of Irish tradition in the bones; an understanding of the language, history and customs, the ballads and poetry, and a great passion for his own place and people, so evident in *Three Villages*. You could not work in his newspaper, as I learned from the day I arrived from Chicago, without deepening your grasp of national identity on a daily basis. At the same time, he was wholly committed to internationalism and to change.

The same apparent contradictions governed his politics. He was a nationalist who loved England and loathed violence. He was an unwavering socialist who couldn't abide left-wing dogmatism, and counted numerous toffs and one or two downright reactionaries among his friends. He was a staunch trade unionist who had furious arguments with Wesley Boyd, then the Father of the Chapel, on an almost weekly basis. He had strong opinions but no difficulty with people who didn't share them, priest or pauper or prince, as long as they held up their end of an argument. His journalism was about debate and democracy, and that too was a daily lesson.

But you wouldn't want to get too solemn. My most abiding memory of Donal as a boss is his abhorrence of pomposity and, even worse, boredom. Inaccuracies made him cross, bad writing made him gloomy, but the reporter who indulged in a sententious comment was risking the worst he could give: uproarious laughter.

As for boredom, his unceasing restlessness in the search for new ideas and new stories drove the paper and all of us who worked there through what were truly wonderful years. If the new appointment we spoke of in July, 2003, does half as much as Donal Foley did, he will be a spectacular success.

Mary Maher 2003.

CHAPTER ONE

S chooldays in Ferrybank were always a mixture of excitement and strange satisfaction and every day seemed to be an adventure in itself. The school had two rooms, a big room where two teachers taught the junior classes, and the gallery, a smaller room with steps right up to the back, where the principal teacher taught. All three teachers were close friends and they always seemed to have a great deal to talk about, particularly on Monday morning when they usually left us to our own devices for about half an hour before they began lessons.

Ferrybank was then a tiny village with one street with the little houses in a row together. The top part of the street was known as the Upper Slip and the lower part, which was closer to the river, was called the Lower Slip. The people were a mixture of dockers, sailors, railway men, factory workers and many unemployed. It was a tight-knit community of less than 600, proud and fiercely tribal with the wives even closer than the husbands. There were no secrets. Both joys and sorrows were shared, and the comradeship which poverty often engenders was strong.

The school presented a fairly accurate reflection of the conditions of the people in that part of Ireland in those years. About a fifth of the boys came to school bare-footed, even in the hardest of winters, boys with pale little faces, dressed in tattered clothes handed down from their brothers. They came from that part of the village where the dockers lived by casual labour.

On arrival at school they were always given special places close to the fire and on wet days their clothing would be steaming. The rest of us in the school were also poorly shod and clothed, as the hand-me-downs were common to us all.

As so many of the fathers in Ferrybank were dockers the river was always watched carefully for the arrival of ships, or the sound of the hooter which signalled their coming. These same ships meant work and porter flowing in Ferrybank's half dozen pubs. When the siren of the coal boats blew in the river all the classroom would be joyful. Next day many boys would come with the ritual note seeking permission to take down their father's dinner to the docks. It was something that, as a child, I always wanted to do. The meal was usually a stew made from the offal that could be purchased cheaply from Clover Meats, the factory in Ferrybank. It was carried down in an old sweet gallon tin and I am sure must have tasted great on the docks.

Looking back on it, that same Waterford river, the Suir, played a very big role in our childhood lives. We learned to swim in it and every summer the river landmarks, the Pier Head, the Ferry Slip and the Ballast Quay became our resorts. It was there, in the early days of June, we had our first swim and experienced the exquisite joy of lying naked on the river bank, basking in the early summer sun.

It was the river Suir that gave Ferrybank its separate identity as a kind of native reservation opposite Waterford city, which we tended to look upon as alien. We thought of ourselves as part of Kilkenny and of the great hurling men of that county. It was the river which divided us. It was a kind of protection and, although we often crossed the bridge or took the Ferry to go to Waterford, we never really felt at home until we were back over the river again.

The fierce tribalism was recognised in the city and in some neighbouring villages, and the saying went "You could walk through Ireland, but you run through the slip

(Ferrybank)." We took it as a just tribute to our tribal abilities.

We were a kind of big family. It was the way the head teacher looked upon us. He was an unusual teacher, determined that school should be an exciting place. Geography, for instance, was taught by making huge sand maps on the school table. We all did it together, and we decided what would represent the rivers, the lakes. We used bits of glass, twine, pieces of chalk and a lump of coal to show where the mines were. To this day I can see Italy as a leg with a shoe on the end of it, and a bone going down the middle.

We learned about all the European countries and Ireland itself in this intimate physical way, but the Inspector never cared that we knew the shape and feel of Europe. If we couldn't rattle off the towns in County Kildare for him, he would tut tut in disapproval. He was shocked when we couldn't tell him where Maynooth was.

The history lessons were taught by linking every townsland in the Parish with a particular period, and we were encouraged to know as much as we could about every area. The Parish of Slieverue and Ferrybank were particularly rich in evocative place names — Rathculliheen, Kilculliheen, Ballinamona, Killaspy, Kilmurry, Attymore, Ballinacrea, Knockane and Newrath. All were pure Irish names with strong historical association with the Pagan and Christian eras, with events and people like John O'Donovan for instance, who translated the Annals of the Four Masters and was born in Attymore.

As well as giving us a strong identity with the area it also gave us deep pride that we were born in such a great little place. Frank Heylin, another of the teachers, did a map of the parish which was illustrated with his own drawings, showing all the associations, historical and cultural. In years gone by the Parish had been part of the Deise, the old tribal Waterford area, a fact that our Irish language loving teachers would not allow us to forget.

Among other subjects taught with great care in Ferrybank School was the gentle art of hurling. Hurling was taught through Irish on the grounds that the language had to be associated with pleasure always. We were shown how to hold a hurley properly, left hand below right; taught how to block an opponent and warned to stand close to an opponent so as to avoid injury. The Teacher's face would glow with pleasure as he demonstrated how to take a seventy. Even then, in his 40s, he had a mighty puck.

Hurling was an important part of the school life in Ferrybank and a hurley was an essential part of the pupil's equipment. We cut down young ash trees, often in the dead of night, and made our own hurleys.

The trees were cut into slabs by workers in Graves' Timber Yard. Each lunch-time we played a match in Pender's field behind the school. Sometimes the farmer who owned, it, who was a cattle dealer from Waterford, would arrive on the scene in the middle of a match and drive us unceremoniously off his land.

Sometimes there would be a shouting match between him and the teacher who took the view that we had a communal right to play on the field anyway. It has since been bought by the local hurling club. Sometimes the teachers would take part in these matches which were played with the ferocity of a championship tie. Many of the same young players went on to become famous Waterford/Kilkenny hurlers.

Timetables and the usual rules of curriculum were never

a strong point in the school. This did not please the Inspector who seemed to take more than a passing interest in Ferrybank's educational matters. He had a habit of bursting in the door and going straight to the timetable to see that we were working to rule. It was rare when we were working to any kind of plan because our teacher usually became so engrossed in a subject that he forgot time. To devote just half an hour to a subject was to him unthinkable. He gave many lectures full of his own philosophy, often straying into politics, religion and even industrial relations in the neighbouring city.

There were always harsh words between the teacher and the Inspector. One day the Inspector was approaching the school at his usual trotting pace and the Teacher locked the door, explaining to him afterwards that we were close to a lunatic asylum and that when he saw a man running towards the school he thought it safer to lock the school.

The Inspector pushed past him and fell down a hole inside the school door which had been there for some months. The school manager had not attended to this matter despite many warnings. The Inspector was caught in the hole, his arms flapping like wings, his face a red glow while we all watched in hysteria, a mixture of fear and elation. The Inspector behaved better after that.

In those days mathematics in the National Schools were not as simple as now. We, for example, did three books of Euclid before we left at 14 and we learned algebra as far as simultaneous equations. We were not a particularly bright bunch, and one of the problems was that working class children could not see these subjects as of practical value. And some of us in today's terms would be classed as slow learners.

The task of the head teacher was how to show us that

what we were learning was practical, and at the same time keep it simple. He consulted the local carpenter, and the wood was cut out in sections we could feel in our hands. For instance, to illustrate an equation like $(x + 3 (x + 4) = x^2 + 7x + 12$ the carpenter cut it all out for us, and we made up the equation on the school table. When theorems were beyond us they were constantly drawn on the black board until eventually we understood. Then we got the same joy from it as we got from our sand maps. I never learned maths afterwards, but those lessons stuck.

Simple interest was taught not by talk of investing money in the banks. We were told to imagine we were going to the local pawnshop, an institution in Waterford well-known to us all. To boys who pawned their fathers' suits every Monday morning until the following Saturday, simple interest became an absorbing reality. So this was how the old kindhearted pawnbroker made his money we thought.

One Mother, who sons were discussing these teaching methods at home, came up to complain. She was sensitive about the fact that they were constant visitors to this same institution. She was met by the teacher at the school door who gave her a hug and told her to go away and have sense. She went down the village saying "You couldn't have a row with that man."

It was just a tribute. He was an extraordinary teacher. He was also my Father.

CHAPTER TWO

"You should never be without a baby in the house," was a favourite saying of my Mother. She, certainly, lived according to her creed, because I can never remember our home ever being without one. She must have practiced some mysterious form of controlled rhythm, because we, all twelve of us, came every two years with the same regularity as the church bells rang out the Angelus in the chapel just below the house in Ferrybank. The local midwife, an elegant woman wearing a dark blue bonnet, would normally come about seven in the evening, and spend the whole time upstairs in the room with Mother. Every so often she would come down for more hot water. Although I was nearly fourteen by the time Mother stopped having babies, I was never aware of what was going on upstairs.

But the next morning there would be a new baby. My Father usually sat up all night smoking his pipe as he sat on a settle bed by the fire. The only difference we noticed was that when we came downstairs for breakfast there was always a big fire in the grate of the range. It was lovely to arrive downstairs to a big warm kitchen. It was usually cold and forbidding in the mornings. My Father would say in Irish – "Go up and see your Mother and see what she has for you." He always spoke Irish to us, and he was proud that we were a bilingual family, and he loved to speak Irish to us. My Mother hadn't much Irish but what she had was genuine Ring Gaeltacht. People were often fooled by her phrases into believing that she was a real native Irish speaker. Upstairs in the bed my Mother would give a wan smile and there would be a baby in the cot, bald and red-faced. They always seemed the same to me, and it never gave me any thrill to see them. The midwife was like a school teacher on these occasions, and she would tell us to be quiet and go downstairs. She wore shapely court shoes, and sheer black stockings like the dancers in the feis. I thought her legs were lovely.

Life in the school house at Ferrybank was eventful. It was a fine big house with four bedrooms upstairs, a big black tiled kitchen downstairs, and a parlour with a hall between. There was a painted picture of my Father's Mother with a deep gilted frame hung over the piano in the corner of the parlour, and my Father would often be found looking at it wistfully. She had died very young, and was very beautiful, and my Father always spoke of her with great warmth and sadness.

Teaching and politics were the passions of my Father's life. He was unfortunate enough to have a very demanding conscience with didn't rest easy in the Ireland of those days when social justice was all too rare. As a very young man he became President of Waterford Workers' Council. He would write out his political speeches, and they were good, tough, socialist utterances, influenced a great deal by James Connolly, the man he admired most of the 1916 leaders. He would write out his political speeches and read them out to my Mother as he walked the kitchen floor. Although she was no politician, he always took great notice of her advice, and the things she had to say about the issues of the day. She acted as a kind of corrective on his more extravagant eccentricities.

One of my Father's particular pleasures was to use the walls of the kitchen as a blackboard. All over the kitchen there would be his chalk drawings, theorems in Euclid, or phrases in Irish that he particularly liked. It seemed that everything he said had to be illustrated, and it became one of the tasks of my Mother's life wiping the walls after his activities. Ideas about everything seemed to pour out of him. He had a practical as well as an artistic side to his nature. For many months he worked quietly on an invention which he eventually modelled and took up to Sean Lemass in Dublin. I think my Mother was glad to see him go up to Dublin one day with the invention in a case. We waited for a result that would make us all wealthy, but it came to nothing. My Father was convinced that one day they would see the value of it. All I know was that it was based on the leverage system, and it took my Father three or four months to assemble it. He saw it as a means of propelling the barges, which in those days were very common on the river Suir.

Father and Mother were very close to Ferrybank, and this was not surprising. Both were born in the village. My Father succeeded his Father as the principal teacher in the little school in Ferrybank. He got the job as a very young man, when he wasn't long out of the de la Salle training college in Waterford. He married his childhood sweetheart Kit who came from a large family, the Powers, who lived in the Cellar. This area was a row of ten three roomed houses overlooking a disused waste ground, and its name had something to do with bacon curing. The waste ground was usually full of stray greyhounds, cats, old bicycles and all sorts of rubbish. The Cellar could not be described as the best area in Ferrybank, but the difference between all areas than was only marginal. Slums had not become known as such, and therefore there was no class consciousness. My Mother had worked in Harvey's Paper Factory for a wage in the region of 5/= a week. Her Father had been killed on the railway working as a shunter. He was caught between the bumpers of two trains, and was carried up to the Cellar to her Mother on an old door, dead. All of her brothers had the option of taking jobs on the railway, which they mostly did, and in the main did very well, two becoming Station Masters. Grandmother Power was a native Irish speaker from Barna, Co. Limerick, and she held very strong beliefs about the freedom of Ireland, which she passed on to her children. The house was a bastion of Republicanism, and a picture of Eamon de Valera always hung on the wall. All the Powers took part in the Civil War – on the Republican side.

My Father and Mother always went for walks in the afternoon, and when my Father went to meetings in Waterford, which he did many nights in the week, they would meet afterwards in her Mother's house in the Cellar to play cards. But the relationship was often tempestuous enough. I think my Mother found it impossible to manage twelve children on a teacher's salary of £24 a month in the thirties. They had to borrow from a Jewish money-lender to pay for second level education. I remember one day when my Mother confessed to my Father that she had not kept up the repayments. He was obviously worried and went a little mad. She was frying the dinner at the time, and my Father took the frying pan full of rashers, eggs and potatoes and threw the lot at the ceiling. The marks remained on the ceiling until we left the house many years later. He regretted it immediately, of course, and there was a warm reconciliation, when we were all told to go and play in the garden. The episode was never mentioned again. I remember some months later, when the Jew called to the house for his money. A pale faced, immaculately dressed and very business like person. I hated the Jews until my Mother told me that the poor man had taken her out of a hole when they needed money, and that he wasn't too bad at all, as moneylenders went. It was a measure of the poverty of the times, however, that people like teachers, who were comparatively well paid, had to resort to this kind of activity, to finance their children's education.

My parents loved the company of everybody in Ferrybank village, and my Father in particular often called in to see a friend Johnny Flynn, who had been a soldier in the Great War, and hear him talk about the horror of the gas attacks. The Great War and that period in particular appalled him and my Father would come home and repeat the stories to my Mother as if they were hot news. Those were the days, of course, when foreign news was a rare commodity.

The radio was largely unknown, and when one came to Ferrybank we were all curious to know what it was like. One of the first to get radio was John Conway, who was married to my Mother's sister. One night my Father took myself and two brothers down to his tiny house in the Lower Slip to hear the wireless. We all sat together with earphones listening to the strange sounds. To me it made no sense at all, just cackling, and a man's voice in the background, but my Father was totally enthralled. He went down night after night to hear the radio, and he came home with the latest news about people killed in earthquakes and changes of Government in foreign countries. I heard him tell my Mother that the wireless would change the world. Things would never be the same again, he said with barely suppressed excitement in his voice.

During the Eucharistic Congress of 1932 all the village assembled in the yard of Pat Shortiss's pub to hear the wireless account from Dublin. The barman was something of an electrical genius, and he had mounted a loudspeaker, so that we were all able to hear rosary after rosary. We were on our knees for hours in the yard in the open air answering the responses. It was like Lourdes at home.

My parents paid one of their rare visits to Dublin for the Congress. My Father used to talk about meeting Tom Shanahan, one of the holiest men in the village, in O'Connell Street in Dublin. Tom said to him, "Dan, if I hear another rosary I'll go mad." One of the memories which my Father had of the Congress was that it was impossible to get a drink in Dublin. He had been calling for a large stout for at least ten minutes over other men's shoulders, but the busy barman did not take any notice. Then he called out somewhat in desperation – "four small stouts and a glass of whisky" and was served immediately. "In Dublin," he used to say, "you have to talk big to get things done."

Just like most villages, ours had its unique people who did not conform, and became accepted institutions of dissent. Such was that lovely strange lady, Miss O'Mara, who was known as the Sheik. There was no explanation for the Ferrybank nicknames, but everyone seemed to have a nickname. Miss O'Mara ran a fruit shop, where everything was incredibly cheap. All the fruit was arranged in glorious disarray, in the front room of one of the little houses which Miss O'Mara would rent to sell that particular lot of fruit. She changed shops with bewildering rapidity, but she was always accepted as a kind of itinerant business woman, and her honesty, even about the smallest things, was legendary.

Her only means of transport was a bicycle. Every morning she rose at dawn, and would got to the Waterford fruit market and take back across the bridge on her bicycle a huge load comprising cases of oranges, boxes of apples, dates and pears. She never accepted assistance, and she

16

would push her bicycle up the steep hill to the top of Ferrybank Cross full of cheerfulness.

She spoke in soft, gentle Limerick tones, and was reputed to be a woman of good education, one of the bacon family in that city. She had pale, distinct features, long tapering fingers. She always dressed in a dirty old mac and she never wore anything but slippers. Her brown straight hair was usually hidden by a bright scarf.

She never spoke of her background, but it was generally assumed that she had broken with the family because of her republican beliefs. She had a reputation of being hard to get on with. We children did not find her so, particularly as she rarely took any money from us. It seemed almost as if she was deliberately providing essential vitamins for the children of Ferrybank.

Every year, without fail Miss O'Mara (we children never referred to her as the Sheik) was arrested for selling Easter Lilies in aid of Republican prisoners. The Guards tended to treat her roughly, perhaps because she was rootless and non conformist. But the sympathies of all the children were firmly on Miss O'Mara's side, and we gladly took up the boxes of lilies, and my Mother always gave us some silver to put in her box. Payment, perhaps, for the free fruit throughout the year. Miss O'Mara never seemed to appear in court because at some stage better counsels would prevail. She was the first protester I ever met, and every time I see Easter Lilies being sold I see the face of that lovely lady.

CHAPTER THREE

The Ireland of the thirties was a very political island, even more so than today, that is, in the southern part. The Civil War hates and loves were still living and strong, no place more so than in small villages where neighbours, thrown together, had taken different sides. Ferrybank was no exception, and like many another village, these hates erupted occasionally on the hurling field, but mostly in the public house. I remember, one day when the Ferrybank hurling team was about to leave in a bus for a match at Moonrue, a group of men came into view on bicycles and one of them shouted as they passed – "Up the blueshirts." Within seconds they were set upon with hurleys and beaten to such an extent that a number were removed to hospital. That episode took place in the mid thirties which was further removed than 1932, the period which made a great impression on my childhood.

The village was largely in favour of de Valera and the 1932 general election provided an ideal opportunity for the people to show their allegiance to the Chief.

My Father had been chosen as the Labour party candidate, so we, as a family, were somewhat removed from the main battle between the supporters of Captain Willie Redmond who was the representative of the Government Party, Cumann na Gael, and Fianna Fáil. Redmond, of course, was something special. He was a son of John Redmond, the Irish leader who had followed Parnell, and who had recruited for the British army in the 1914 war. The Redmondite tradition in Waterford was strong. It had been strengthened further by the fact that so many young Waterford men had died in Flanders for what they saw as the Redmond cause. To the Republicans the name of Redmond was an anathema. It was a brave man indeed, who stepped into this cauldron of barely muted hate.

Both Irish leaders, the President of the executive council as he was then Mr. W.T. Cosgrave, and Mr. Eamon de Valera, did national tours. Mr. De Valera held meetings all over the country, often talking in blinding rain and holding ten or fifteen thousand people. The Waterford meeting was the greatest political gathering that I have ever seen. On a cold, dark night Dev was met about a mile from the city boundary on the New Ross road where we lived. Six bands including Ferrybank's own pipers and hundreds of people carrying blazing lights on tall poles greeted the Chief. A bodyguard of horsemen accompanied the open carriage to which he had been transferred.

Earlier in the day my Mother had confronted my Father with the news that she would like to honour Dev's visit to Waterford by decorating the house in some way. Her old loyalty was too strong to throw overboard, even when her husband was a Dáil candidate opposing Dev's party. "Do what you like, Kit," he told her gently. And she consulted us, and then, as darkness fell, we saw what she had been thinking about. She took out a packet of candles and put many lines of them all alight, in the four large windows in front of the house. The house looked like a huge square shrine shining in the darkness, and de Valera could not miss it.

The Fianna Fáil candidate in Waterford, Paddy Little, who was in the carriage with Dev, reported later to my Mother that Dev had asked him about the lighted windows, and when told that they belonged to one of the opponents in election, he replied, "that's why outsiders will never understand Irish politics."

That same night the road outside our house was thick with big shadowy figures. One heard voices and saw the heads and the faces, but they were all blurred in the darkness. When the torch carriers arrived over the hill to herald the arrival of de Valera, every throat in South East Ireland seemed to open up with shouts of friendly welcome. Excitement seemed to surge through the crowd, and when Dev passed our house my normally quiet Mother called out Up Dev in a very loud voice. And the great man stood bareheaded and waved over at our shrine. The huge concourse of dark figures moved slowly past our house and was passing for fully an hour with the music of the bands dominating over all the usual night sounds of birds and animal cries. A few nights later W.T. Cosgrave came in from Kilkenny direction, and we also had a big torchlight procession and many bands. Captain Willie Redmond sat with Mr. Cosgrave and the Ballybricken women with shawls on their heads, many of them war widows, were there in their thousands to roar "Up Redmond". It was really Willie Redmond's night.

I began to feel sorry for my Father and apprehensive, too, that he would be badly beaten by the men from the big parties. We did not want him disgraced. His meeting in Ferrybank, however, cheered us all no end. Earlier in the day the boys of the school had collected bracken and timber from the woods round Ferrybank and when the meeting was due to start they had a huge bonfire blazing at the Cross at the top of the village, and the Ferrybank band played "Wrap the Green Flag round me, Boys" before the meeting. All the village turned out to greet him and when he stood up to speak they cheered him for fully five minutes. As always he spoke first in Irish about the people of Ferrybank and a number of them understood him too, for he had seen to that by his teaching of Irish in the school up the road. In English he hammered home his somewhat prosaic message of jobs, houses and better education for the worker's child.

Of course he did not win the election, but he got nearly four thousand votes, which was amazing in the context of those times, when the Civil War issues were so alive. A few more votes would have got him elected, and I discovered that he was very disappointed. He had been quietly confident, and so were the organised workers in the City and Dungarvan who had strongly supported him, but he had given the parties a rare fright and he was proud of the fact that some twelve hundred voters had plumped for him, that is they had given him their Number One vote and did not use the other preference votes to which they were entitled.

A few years later the village was involved in other excitements, this time an industrial dispute which had grave repercussions on the whole community. That same strike in the local bacon factory, Clover Meats, which is now a flourishing concern, is worth recalling in some detail because it did show the strong bonds and the great sense of social justice which bound that little riverside community together. Clover Meats was the only real factory in Ferrybank. It was known simply as the Factory, and was owned in co-operative style by the farmers of Kilkenny and South Tipperary. It was to this factory or the docks and railways that most Ferrybank boys went to work.

When the factory opened the oldest boys in the school went there as the pioneer workers. A number left immediately because they couldn't stand the smell of the pigs, the gutting and the various processes which the product went through, before finding its way as hams and sides of bacon and sausages to various parts of Ireland and Britain.

The Factory was ideally situated on the banks of the Suir in surroundings of rich grass and woods, about half a mile south of Ferrybank. It was also served by rail and road as well as the river.

The strike which took place in the early thirties was about the old basic issue of trade union recognition, which was not uncommon in those days. When the strike began, it seemed to us children a lighthearted affair. It meant that our hurling team was much fuller than usual, as the young strikers availed of the opportunity to practise for the forthcoming Waterford championship games. We felt that, of course it was only a misunderstanding and they would be back at work very soon. But then dark rumours began to circulate about new young men arriving to work at the factory from North Kilkenny and South Tipperary. Only too soon the rumours were confirmed and the next thing we heard was that an old disused mansion near the factory was being used as a hostel, where they could live while they took up the jobs of the Ferrybank strikers. The management of the factor was stubborn. The Chairman of the Board of Directors was a Cumann na nGael T.D. named Denny Gorey, a tough, rough-tongued man, who had plenty of courage and was determined to win the strike. He saw it simply as a betrayal of the farmers.

The strikers, who were members of the Amalgamated Transport and General Workers' Union, held a meeting in Waterford to get local support. The Ferrybank band, our own village combination of pipers and drummers, assembled at the village crossroads and played our national anthem, Ferrybank Boys Hoorah. We had our own version:

"On the top of Fleming's Knock, we will make the pig buyers hop, and they'll never see ould Ireland any more." People in the village marched into town behind the band and supported the strikers. My father was the principal speaker, and he warned that workers living in hostels meant the breakup of family life. "This is communism on our doorstep," he said. It was a very effective stick with which to beat management in those days.

The next Sunday, the blacklegs were escorted to Mass by the Gardai. They marched at each side of the men in formation, and as they marched, all the children stood and jeered at them and sang "You're in the army now, you're not behind the plough". The latter was a reference to the fact that they were all the sons of strong farmers.

As the strike went on and on fear and bitterness gripped the strikers and their families. The lorries carrying products to the station from the factory were stoned. Then the porters at the station would not handle the goods, the factory men had to come and do it themselves. There were rumours of sausages being left to rot at the factory. My Father made an official complaint about the smell, which he said was a health hazard to the pupils at the school. One night the blacklegs were escorted to a local pub by the local Gardai for drinks. All the local men left.

A woman whose son had decided to return to work at the factory told a passing farmer what she called "her good news". The farmer, Larry Walsh, grunted and said "I don't want to know anything about your blood money ma'am," adding as an afterthought, "Didn't you do the same to Parnell". The folk memory is a long one in village life. Another local man who had broken on the strike lived in a remote area. Gardai accompanied him to his home, but they allowed him to walk up the last twenty yards to his home in a lane. Two strikers were concealed in the lane and set upon the man and beat him up.

So the bitterness continued, with a few local men who had gone back to work being boycotted in Land League fashion.

There was joy unconfined in Ferrybank when the local team won the minor hurling championship, short of three stars who had blacklegged in the strike. There was no question of inviting them to play. The bonfires blazed that night in the Slip and the porter flowed.

The strike wore on for weeks, and the factory kept going somehow, but the heart was torn out of the strikers, and some were hungry too. Eventually a clergyman stepped in an negotiated some kind of settlement. There would be recognition for the union, but the management were allowed to pick the men to go back. A vote was taken, and by some means or other a narrow majority was achieved. Many strikers were very bitter about it.

A number of the Ferrybank strikers were not rehired, and they left to work in a bacon factory in Acton in London, where a former friendly Clover man was manager. Most of them never came back and the village was much the poorer for it. But the factory went on and prospered and became fully unionized, and the bulwark of the economy in a larger and more modern village. The strikers lost the immediate battle, but they laid the foundations. They should not easily be forgotten.

CHAPTER FOUR

Every year, during the second week of July, the Foley family went to Ring, Co. Waterford, for six weeks holiday. It had been the custom since my Father and Mother got married, and it was maintained all our lives.

I was born there, in the year 1922 during the Civil war. We were unable to return because of the conflict, and eventually, the Mother and young baby came home by sea from Helvick Head to Waterford. Ring is the place in Ireland that I really love the best. Its fields, thatched houses and craggy cliffs have been with me all my life. The people when I was a child lived in a world of the sea, fishermen and fishing, told each other strange stories about ghosts and the things the sea did to them.

I looked forward to that journey to Ring every year, and to my Father it seemed like the fulfillment of an annual dream. We were the only people in Ferrybank who had a holiday at all, and it was due to the ingenious and cheap way it was all planned. These journeys to Ring were something always to remember, particularly at a time when private cars were unknown in the village. The journey every year dominated our childhood years like a pilgrimage. We talked about it for months before the great day arrived, and when it was gone, we remembered it as people nowadays discuss journeys to America. To us children that forty mile trip provoked all the excitement that Concorde must do now to adults.

There were fourteen of us and we travelled by open lorry, except my Mother who sat with the driver with a baby in her arms in the front seat. The lorry which was known as the "Linnet" in the Ring Co-op to which it belonged would arrive outside our gate at about mid-day. We would all be up early, crazy with excitement having watched from very early at the gate for its arrival. It was a grey, battered old Ford, but it had a great engine which we knew had the power to get us anywhere. There was no need to pack as nothing could be done until the lorry arrived. When the mattresses and springs were carried into the lorry, and laid on the floor, that was the foundation. Then everybody in the house helped, and all the village children as well. One child carried a pet, another a pan, another a bundle of napkins. There were overcoats, bathing togs, bundles of shoes, and a rabbit in a cage. Between the gate and the hall door the constant procession of carriers went on for about forty minutes. It was assumed, eventually, that everything was packed somewhere in the lorry. Then came the big moment when my Father came behind the big lorry and helped us all in. When we were all aboard, my Father would heave his own seventeen stone up to sit in the middle. Then, like some great Emperor on his throne, he commanded the driver – "Anois a Thomais". Then a shrill cry from my Mother in the front – "Dan, is the kettle in and the door locked?" He would unlock the door, and usually find the kettle on the hob, singing away. A little later, he would emerge with the kettle in a bag. Back on his throne, and again the driver would start.

It was not a non-stop journey. There were various landmarks where we halted. Father and the driver disappeared for a few minutes, sometimes longer. They always came back with lemonade and I remember the first discordant note entered when we had had a fight over who should get the longest drink.

The older ones knew the road well and they indulged in a sort of "one-upmanship" by calling out the names of the villages. The Sweep, Ballyduff, the Pike and Abbeyside. To us younger ones everything, although vaguely familiar, still had the fascination of the unknown. Things seemed bigger and different than at home. Even the cows were larger.

The big moment came when we caught sight of the sea. This was the signal that we were coming to the end of the journey. Across the sea was the jutting peak of Helvick head and between, the great expanse of Dungarvan Bay.

However, there were still some delights of the journey to come. The square in Dungarvan with its carts and knots of people talking. They stared curiously at us as our lorry drove resolutely through. Then the road by the rim of the bay and the twisting winding hill that ended at the sea in Ballinagoul. The village was in readiness for us. Big fishermen with large red weather-beaten hands and black jerseys lifted us down from the lorry and solemnly shook our hands and a hundred willing helpers carried our things into our cottage. Finally the lorry was empty and it started again with a great cracking noise and chugged away up the village. We watched it in the twilight until it rounded the bend and we knew the journey was over for another year.

Ring was another world where people always spoke in Irish, a world of men with thick black jerseys and brown faces, the same colour as the rocks at Faill an Staichin, the dangerous rocky cliff which we climbed down every day to swim and bask on the lovely hot strand. A strand which was always washed with mountainous waves. The strand was enclosed by the high cliffs, rocks and deep ravines where the water swirled in and out all day long.

What made Ring a garden of adventure for us children was that the houses were placed haphazardly in tiny townlands with a fine disregard for the planners, far in from the road. The houses were linked by a series of mysterious pathways which went through fields at various angles.

Suddenly, after walking on a pathway bounding a field of oats you came upon a tiny hamlet where there would be men talking of the night's fishing as they smoked their pipes on the grassy verge.

The fields were of all shapes and sizes, some three-cornered and square, others half-circular. The shapes were hammered out by previous generations of Ring men after days of hard bargaining and landlordism. Each little field had its own name and meant much to its owner not only because it meant food but it also meant land.

The fishermen were mostly small men with friendly, twinkling eyes and they seemed to have all day to talk to us and answer our many questions. They seemed so different from their wives, who were always busy boiling potatoes, washing or feeding the hens. We didn't know then that the men had been out fishing during the night, and were lying around relaxing, and the wives were doing all the work of an Irish wife, living in a thatched cabin with no mechanical aids but her two strong hands. In Ballinagoul where we lived, all the houses were thatched except for two or three built by the Council, which were slated. The floors of the thatched houses were uneven and sloped down to the front door. The table was balanced by stones and the dresser as well. The fire built up with turf and stoked faithfully all day by the housewife was an open one and you could see the sky through the chimney. There was normally a wheel which when turned drove the flames up the chimney. A settle bed, a big dresser with patterned plates, a table, a couple of wooden chairs and a stool. We knew all the houses intimately, because only the half doors were closed, and people walked in and out of each other's houses as if they were communally owned. An old man or woman might come in, sit on the settle and gaze into space without saying a word, and then leave in silence. But this was unusual, for they were garrulous people and usually had many interesting things to talk about.

At mealtimes there was always an invitation to sit up to the table. We children always accepted and we distributed our custom over all the village. We loved every mouthful because it was away from home. The meals were always the same. A big pile of spuds in the middle of the table, bursting in their jackets, boiled mackerel on a plate in the middle also and buttermilk. You helped yourself until you were full. We always praised the spuds because my Mother told us it was courteous to the man and woman of the house. The man and wife usually set the potatoes together in the Spring.

Ferrybank never seemed so friendly again after our experience of Ring. Although the lives in both villages were hard. In Ring they fished in small open sailing boats in bad weather and good, and with no proper protective clothing, for fish such as mackerel, whiting and sand dabs. Some had lobster pots. All were sold to a gombeen man in Dungarvan for a mere pittance. There were family boats, others were fished by groups of men, one or two had big old fashioned sailing boats and a crew of five or six. The floors of these boats were usually full of ballast, gravel and sand.

Every night during the summer months at about five o'clock in the evening, the men would go down to the pier at Ballinagoul or Helvick, clutching their little parcels of bread and a bottle of milk. Those mid-summer nights, the sky over Dungarvan Bay with the dark Comeraghs in the background, was a blaze of magnificent bright red and the little boats going out to sea at Helvick Head over towards Ballinacourty or Stradbally were being given it seemed, a great nostalgic warm farewell. The sunset often lasted as long as two hours. The boats would be back at dawn and the crunch of the boots of the men coming up from the pier would be the only sound in the sleeping village, except for the bawling of the donkeys, which never seemed to stop. At night, when the men were out the candles shining through the tiny little windows were the only signs of life in the lonely village street. The waiting wives baked and blew the fire to heat the covers of the pot oven. Few of them ever purchased bread.

But then Friday nights when the men were not out fishing there would be a ceilí when we would all assemble in Ally's house, because her son Cud played the flute. And there was a tiled floor in a good expanse of kitchen were the sets could be danced. The boys and girls sat on stools and boxes by the walls and they watched the old woman blow the fire. One would not dare start the dancing before she decreed it. The ritual was always the same. There would be many hints dropped before she would ask her son to play, and then she would say, almost accusingly "Cad margheall ar an gceoil?" (what about the music?) Within seconds the floor would be full of lively men and women dancing sets as if their lives depended upon it.

The dancing was really a kind of endurance test, and each couple seemed to dance faster and faster. The dresser, the chairs and the people all became blurred eventually. Outside in the dark street people gazed in through the half door. We children watched it all enthralled. Then there would be singing. Songs that were indigenous, written by men long since dead, about the deeds of men who revolted against the landlords, like the Connerys, or Sliabh na mBan (the Mountain of the Women) a song of the 1798 revolution. They all spoke and sang in Irish. They were really one family.

CHAPTER FIVE

In Ring, in those years of the thirties, had we but known it, we were watching and taking part in the dying years of an ancient culture. Ring was a unique situation, a little tiny peninsula stretching out on the west side of Dungarvan Bay into usually turbulent seas. A place cut off from the rest of West Waterford where the people spoke the language of old Ireland and were part of a culture that had died in the large area of West Waterford which had been Irish-speaking a few short years previously. In Ring, their particularly hard and communal way of life, fishing and small farming, had helped them to preserve a kind of island identity, but it was not in any sense a conscious kind of survival. The people in their rich innocence were not even aware of any special quality in their way of life. To them it was all as natural as the tiny winding corkscrew roads and hills which, while contributing to their isolation, were too the tenuous link which bound them to the land. These were days when cars, and travel as we know it today, only forty short years later in the century, were completely unknown. The isolation and the constant close links with the elements contributed to the fact that the five or six hundred people huddled together in the collection of houses dotted through the little hamlets were totally different from the people of our own village at home.

The Boy Buidhe was in many ways the kind of man that was a product of that society. In his old age, when we knew him, he was a little sad but always kind to us. Every day he sat on the little stone wall which ran down the length of Ballinagoul, separating it from the strong running stream. At the other side of the stream which was about 4ft. lower then the village proper was a little lane and a line of cottages thatched and yellow coloured, and in those years housing about a dozen families. That stone wall was used to dry nets, and also to dry the mackerel and herrings which were laid out on the wall with hard salt rubbed into them. After a day in the hot sun they would be picked by the women and packed in little wooden barrels for preservation, to be eaten in the winter months when there would be no fishing. The Boy Buidhe was always dressed in a big black fisherman's jersey, and a rough tweed trousers, hobnailed boots and a slouched hat pulled down on his head. He was a big portly man, overweight then, but one could sense the strength that was once in his big bones. He did not often speak, but his big sallow face always creased into a smile when we sat with him on the wall. When the fishermen went out to fish in the evenings, we knew he was sad he couldn't go. Sometimes he would talk to us of fishing and tell us all the places he had fished, and the boatmen he knew. He was a lonely man and he lived in a tiny house in the middle of the village. All his days were spent on that wall until it came to 6 o'clock in the evening, when he would go for his bottle of milk.

We were always asking him questions and we never expected a reply. But we found out from neighbours how he got his name. When he was very young he had a shock of golden hair, and a doting mother who always referred to him as her Boy Buidhe – my yellow boy. When the Bishop, on Confirmation Day asked him his name he had replied Boy Buidhe, and so the name had remained, I remember we used to hope that some day he would have a boat again, and we would all go with him fishing, because we knew he was the best fisherman in Ring.

One day, and I remember it well, the Boy Buidhe

amazed us by constant questions, asking us about Waterford and the motor cars and the buses, and then finally he blurted out a question. "Are you going to town on Saturday in the bus?" It was the first we had heard of the bus, and we were just as excited about it as the Boy Buidhe. We told Mother about it and she decided she too would go to town on that bus. That day the Boy Buidhe was not in his accustomed place. From early morning the old man, dressed in his Sunday best suit of blue serge and striped woolen shirt with a stud, was up at the Cross, waiting for the bus. He sat on the ditch unusually talkative, greeting the neighbours in his rich Irish, as they joined the crowd. When the bus came he was the first to go aboard and nobody dreamed of going ahead of him. He sat in the front seat just near the driver. It was clear that his role was almost as important as the man behind the wheel. On reaching Dungarvan he sat in Grattan Square, one of the loveliest squares in Ireland, watching the people from the country bringing in their produce. They chatted in groups and the Boy Buidhe would join in with the Irish speakers. He was first on the bus going home, and every Saturday from then on he made that journey into Dungarvan, occupying the same seat in the bus. During the week he would tell us about the people he had met from Aglish, Coolnahorna and Kilcash, the small villages of West Waterford. Everybody who would pass down the street would be asked if they were going to town next Saturday. Then when people began to know he always went on the bus, they began to ask him to get messages. Finally, he was doing messages for everybody, and he was the happiest man in Ballinagoul, because he was wanted again. My Mother always said that it was the bus that made the Boy Buidhe a happy man again.

Oddly enough, perhaps more symbolic then real, it was the same bus that heralded the end of the Ring that I remember of fiercely independent tribal people. A community that drew strength from its own size, but in the end it was because of its smallness that it could not exist in isolation. In a small community characters like the Boy Buidhe etched themselves on childhood memories and became larger than life. I remember Larry Mhaire Nell who had fought in World War I and who never tired of telling us of the battles he had won, but particularly of the Jarman (German) whom he had at his mercy, "My bayonet was at his throat, and he screamed out for mercy," Larry told us, and we hung on his every word. Then a pause for breath, and Larry, with his stick for bayonet demonstrated how he stuck the bayonet through the heart of the German with the harsh parting words, "Too late a fhir bhocht." We never tired of that demonstration, and Larry always forgot that he had told us this story before.

My Father and Mother loved the beautiful townslands of Ring like Ceann A'Mhacalla where no one knew English and the Irish had a special pure quality and the people too. We would all set out on a high summer's day to Faill an Staichin or a visit to Peggy Finger. This was not her real name of course, but Ring names took a great deal of unraveling, as everybody was related. Peggy, who was an old woman herself, lived with two aged brothers on the Langwee, the cliffs overlooking the sea at the south of Ring. Peggy always gave us buttermilk to drink, and praised us in turn, before guiding us over the correct tiny paths along the dangerous cliffs to Kelly's house in Ceann A'Mhacalla. This house, one of a cluster set along the clifftop fields by the rim of the ocean was always full of gaiety, and the Kellys, parents and children, loved to see my Father and Mother and all of us. Polly Kelly sang the lovely indigenous songs of the neighbourhood, which recounted history, and history enhanced by local participation. I always understood that the famous Connery brothers of Ring's most famous song came from this townsland, but seemingly they did not, but from Modeligo. Then there were, of course, other and similar revolutionaries all over the Déise. The other favourite townsland was Seana Chill where I was born in Deuglan Griffin's cottage. It was an area of the same kind, very rich in songs and folklore, but not as isolated. There were always roads going through it. It was here that Deuglan Regan, my God-father, lived, and his wife Peg. There was always a celebration in this area, no doubt my parents remembering a great event.

To us young children Dave the Prophet, who lived at the top of the cliff in Ballinagoul, in a house falling down around him, was the most fascinating character of all. We were afraid of him, yet about once a week we would pay him a ritual visit, unknown to our parents. Dave tarred his skin to keep out the cold and he ignored the seasons, planting seeds at all times of the year, and oddly enough with some success. He never went near the local church, but conducted his own religious services in the darkness of his tiny cabin. He slept during the day, and he walked the roads at night, with a huge staff. He fished the cliffs at night, and brought home Pollock and mackerel. He believed he was capable of controlling the elements, and at night he would leave his cottage and go to the top of the cliff. There, he would stand and blow his foghorn commanding the sea and the winds to cease. Sometimes my Father would put his head out of the window and tell him to have sense and go back to sleep. But that was rare as the foghorn was accepted as one of the night sounds of sea.

Dave, unlike most people in Ring, spoke perfect English, and used unusual words. He had been to America and would sometimes take the trouble of telling us all about that country. But he never regretted coming home to the life of a hermit. For he firmly believed that the whole place belonged to him alone, and he got great joy as a result of walking his land. Before his death he was persuaded to go to hospital, and was reconciled like everybody else to the old traditions. A Ring woman who went in to see him told the neighbours that he looked "like a new quart in the bed".

This was the period when the Irish revival movement was at its height, and the Irish College in Ring was the center of much of that movement. Hundreds of scholars from all over the country came to it, and they swarmed all over the place, taking notes and talking to the mystified Ring people. For some reason they were known as the Gabricks. They were treated with great affection, but were generally regarded as slightly eccentric. The village, of course, supplied its own quota of teachers to the Institution, but the College, strangely enough, was never really a part of the people's lives. It was, nevertheless, a thriving college, and if the place is remembered it will be because of that Institution. It is sad, though, that the village declined and its people went into exile, while the culture which they represented was cherished behind the walls of Colaiste na Rinne. The failure of the Revival Movement in the end is not unconnected with that odd fact.

CHAPTER SIX

The school retreat remains a searing memory of an intensely militant occasion, but without any of the competition or the love that was so much a part of our young lives in other ways. Father Mackey, a priest in his late fifties or early sixties gave the retreat and I suspect he regarded his role as that of a cleansing one – he cast out the devils from the boys of Ferrybank.

The Parish Priest, Father Edward Brennan, a kindly old man who spent every afternoon in Ferrybank Church, always gave us advance warning of the retreat and it was clear that he regarded us as being highly privileged because the great Father Mackey was coming to Ferrybank. He was indeed famed all over Ireland for the same retreats.

The first night Father Mackey would come in his black soutane and cap and sit intimately on the school table where he gave us a short gallop over the course, as it were. This introductory sermon simply told us that the next week we would spend "working on our knees for Christ," and when Father Mackey said "working on our knees" he meant just that. Every boy was expected to do the stations at least twice, say about four rosaries, go to Mass, Communion and Benediction every day. There was a sermon every morning and also one every evening. It was clear from the start that Father Mackey knew exactly what we were all thinking about.

He seemed to have X-ray eyes which saw right into our minds, so that we could hardly stir a muscle while the persuasive heavy voice went on relentlessly, accusing us all of dreadful crimes against our own bodies. Then the voice would rise to a crescendo of passion. "In the body of an athlete you can have the soul of a weakling, while in the poor crippled weak hungry body you can have a soul that is strong and getting closer to Christ. If there is any boy here in mortal sin – let him come straight to me and confess his sins and get rid of the monster".

Father Mackey clearly believed that all boys were totally preoccupied with sex. "Impurity will bring you down to the depths," he would shout, in a thunderous voice, while we all sat frightened out of our very lives, trembling, uncomprehending and bewildered.

These sermons were delivered in the comparative intimacy of the school where we were close enough to feel the priest's own passion. He was no actor but a deadly sincere man determined to give us a week of militant Christianity on our knees. Confession was, of course, a vital part of the mission, and it was intimidatingly intimate. Father Mackey sat on a chair in the smaller schoolroom and we all went in our turn to confess. We knelt on the floor at his feet while he sat on a chair, sometimes holding our hands in his hands – probing – probing –

"Sins of the front now, my boy,"

"What do you mean, Father?"

"Did you get pleasure from that thought?"

"Did you allow it to stay in your mind?"

So the insistent voice went on and on, exploring the most intimate feelings, suggesting, suggesting, until finally you had told every detailed thought that ever entered your mind. Totally free from it all you left Confession feeling cleansed, determined to work for Christ. A little soldier fully fledged. Father Mackey had won his battle against Satan.

One night in the middle of a sermon the Preacher suddenly stopped, and in a low-pitched voice demanded,

"Is there any boy in the school who has not gone to Confession?" We all sat guilty and silent, for we all knew that there was one boy who had not. Afterwards a group of us conferred and decided that the priest should know that Peter had not been to Confession. We could not have him full of sins among us Soldiers of Christ. We watched the priest call around to the unfortunate boy's home and walk him up to Confession in the little room. Everyone was happy.

Religion generally was a form of discipline. We went to Holy Communion on the second Sunday of every month. Every Communion Sunday a boy from the Lower Slip collapsed and my Father carried him out. The sermons were normally reminders of the rules which were constantly broken except when Father Murphy, the curate, preached, and he would speak at great length of the Virgin Mother, whom he quite clearly believed was his real Mother. He spoke always with tremendous sentimentality of the great favours which she had achieved for him, and one felt that all was not discipline and rules. The Virgin Mother would be kind and helpful.

But the rules were still important even to Father Murphy. Once when a local Protestant landowner died who was also a doctor and kind to the people we children went along to the funeral at the Abbey Church. This was the local Church of Ireland establishment which the wealthy Protestants in the neighbourhood attended every Sunday like exclusive brethren. The only traffic jams I can remember as a child were outside that same church.

We went to the funeral out of respect, but also because we wanted to known what the church was like inside. Of course we did not recognize it as a church at all, but as a kind of mumbo-jumbo museum. That day we saw hundreds of men from the British Legion carrying wreaths and wearing medals like we saw at Captain Willie Redmond's funeral a few years earlier. When we went to Confession, though, the important thing from Father Murphy's point of view was, had we heard the words of the Minister at the funeral. We certainly had heard the words of the Minister at the funeral. We certainly had heard the hymns. But had we taken part, Father Murphy asked. We didn't know whether we had or not. Our Curate was undecided, so, as attending Protestant services was a reserved sin in the Diocese of Ossory, we had to wait until the Bishop gave Father Murphy permission before we got forgiveness. It meant waiting a fortnight before the magic words were conveyed to us. I have never been in such a sinful predicament since then.

Confirmation Day was the great religious landmark in the lives of young people in our village. It was a great communal occasion with all of us wearing new suits, and the girls in white veils and bouquets of Lily of the Valley. It was a great day to remember ages by when one got older. "Oh, she made her Confirmation with me." There were few festival days in those years, and Confirmation was certainly one of them. It took place every three years and everyone took the day off.

The day before, the stall people who sold rosary beads, holy water fonts, white prayerbooks and medals and badges of all shapes and sizes, would set up their canvas shops outside the chapel gates. They did a roarin' trade, and the Bishop always asked the people to hold up the religious objects to be blessed. The medals, prayerbooks and all the trinkets would be held up while His Lordship pronounced the blessings. The coming of the Bishop was like the visit of a prince. He always looked majestic with his mitre and crozier and expensive, colourful vestments. When he advanced up the aisle blessing the people the whole parish, men, women and children, would be on their knees wrapped in devotion. The Bishop gave a sermon in which he congratulated the priest on the spiritual state of the parish.

For the children, who had been cramming Schuster's Bible History, the Green Catechism and the red Catechism, the confirmation examination was an awful ordeal. Groups of children formed a half-circle around the Bishop's throne, and he asked them questions in stentorian tones while the whole parish listened. One young boy, asked to state what was the greatest misfortune which could befall a person, replied, "Extreme poverty". The shocked Bishop refuted him immediately and told him that mortal sin was the correct reply. When it came to my own question I got an attack of a recurring nervous trouble and my mouth simply refused to function. The parish priest explained and I was passed over. I felt that all the parish had their eyes on me and only made my way back to my seat with the greatest of difficulty. I sat down deeply humiliated and was certain that I had failed the examination and let my Father down in front of the whole parish. Worst of all I would not be confirmed at all. I need not have worried, however, and the next day I was made a strong and perfect Christian like the rest. But the memory of that day stays with me always.

The Confraternity on Sunday nights was another ritual exercise which was a vital part of our religious life as older school-boys. Normally it consisted of the Rosary, Benediction, hymn-singing and a sermon. Once a month the Holy Hour was held, and on these nights the devotions were extended to last about an hour and twenty minutes.

This was an exercise to be avoided at all costs, and usually was by a sudden desire to do the homework from school. That night there would be Latin, History and all sorts of copybooks spread out on the kitchen table. It was an impressive academic sight, but it rarely fooled my Mother. I think she just liked the sight of books on the table.

For the Confraternity, the parish was divided behind various banners or guilds, and everyone was always in great singing voice. It was great to observe the intensity of feeling as voices rose to a tremendous crescendo in unison for "God Bless Our Pope" or "To Jesus' Heart All Burning With Fervent Love Of Men". It was a rare opportunity for self-expression, when people could give vent to their real feelings. I actually enjoyed being in the church for these occasions, but because we were told to be there we avoided it if at all possible. It was vitally important not to meet one of the priests as you went on the road to Waterford for the pictures. If you did there would be questions and lying excuses which always left a resentful feeling against the priests. You felt that what you did with your own time was your own business, but it was seldom that you had the courage to say so at that young age. More's the pity – it would have done the priest good also.

CHAPTER SEVEN

My Father went to Dublin on a winter morning in 1936 to see a specialist for his health, and I carried his case to the station. He wore a dark heavy overcoat which the Parish Priest, Fr. Brennan, had given him and insisted he should wear on the cold journey to Dublin. Father had no overcoat of his own.

We spoke little, and I felt ill at ease and worried because I knew he was going up to Dublin for a serious operation. For months past in the middle of class he would suddenly stop teaching, his face contorted with pain, and hold the table. 'Those oul pains again, boys,' he would say, and after a minute he would continue his lesson in the old eager tones. At the station that day my Father shook my hand formally and said goodbye. I never saw him in his health again, and he came home six months later, his great frame wasted with cancer.

In Dublin he had undergone an operation which lasted four hours for stomach cancer, and he had never really recovered. He died on 20th July, 1937, a few weeks after another turbulent general election de Valera's government had won again. The Labour Party in Waterford had nominated him to the Dáil in spite of his illness. Although my Father had never campaigned at all he got more than 3,000 votes, which was regarded by everyone as a demonstration of personal respect and affection.

His funeral was a great tribal day of mourning. It took place from Ferrybank Chapel-of-Ease to Slieverue, the neighbouring village about a mile and a half away in the same Parish. Schoolboys lined the route in Slieverue and Ferrybank and the people marched all the way. The funeral was fully that mile and a half long. His comrades in the Labour movement carried the coffin first, and then they handed it to the teachers who bore it on their shoulders to the grave. It was a great occasion, and I remember feeling very insecure and alone.

In spite of all the tedious ritual the Irish funeral does have a comforting effect. The words spoken at the graveside, even the unspoken sorrow of the old grave digger who truly knew him from cradle to grave, was deeply moving. Dan Callaghan, A T.D. in the first Dáil, spoke a panygeric, and reminded us of his courage and idealism and dramatically saluted his old comrade at the close. We all cried profusely and left Slieverue lonely and broken-hearted. After all he was only fifty, and it seemed terribly unjust on that summer's day.

The thirties in Ireland was a time of much poverty for most people. Unemployment was the normal state, and a harbour such as Waterford dependent on the Anglo-Irish trade suffered heavily from the economic war which followed the refusal of the Irish Government to pay the land annuities. The people in our village, although they suffered on the docks particularly supported de Valera, nevertheless on his stand. But there was much confusion around; the Republican movement had split into left and right factions and the Blue Shirts, a right wing farmers' organization, sons of the men who had taken the pro-treaty stand in the Civil War, were drilling openly. Their leader, the ex Garda Chief Eoin O'Duffy, had made foolish speeches which had undertones of the demonic stupidities of the dictators Mussolini and Hitler, who at that time were solidly building up their bases in Europe. The Spanish Civil Ward had added to the confusion, with Catholic leaders appealing for support for Franco, and the

45

republicans calling for support for the Government. Eventually, we saw the spectacle of two Irish brigades going to Spain on different sides. The Republican side included an old friend of the family, Frank Edwards, a Waterford national teacher. The death of my father had changed things dramatically for our family, still largely unprovided for. Teachers' widows in those bad days had no special pension except the salary of £300 for one year. We had to leave the official school residence and ended up finally in a new Corporation Estate which had been added to the old village in the building programme of the forties. The house was tiny and inadequate for our size of family. My mother kept us at school because she used to say 'education will never be a burden to you'. It was her old fashioned Irish country woman's belief that somehow or some way there would be light at the end of a tunnel for those who were well equipped with the rudiments of education, and she was right. We boys were sent to St. Patrick's College, a secondary school run by the de La Salle brothers where the fees were £3.00 a year. Brother Edmund, a friend of my Father insisted on paying my fee. That school, mercifully for us at least, was not of the competitive kind that was so common in Ireland, and understandable too in those days of little opportunity. The inter-cert and the leaving cert. results from the two rival schools were published in full in Waterford papers, but St. Patrick's was a delightful, lackadaisical place which did not adhere to such alien practices. The students were a motley collection, mainly of the working class and farming communities from the villages of Kilmacow, Mulinavat, Slieverue in Kilkenny and Ballyduff, Butlerstown, and Passage in Waterford. This rural collection was leavened with city slickers, of whom we were beginning to count ourselves, from the great metropolis of Waterford. One local woman confused my Mother by describing the school derisively to her as the farmers' College. She meant a school for country yokels.

The building was a converted graceful, merchant style house in Newtown on the southern fringe of the city by the river bank. The school had vast grounds extending down to the river including gardens and two small playing fields. Part of the grounds were marshland which, in a reclamation scheme, were used as a city dump. The smell from the dump, plus the sewage from the Suir at low tide was not always pleasant, but we were a gay, carefree lot and pollution did not worry us. We, the Ferrybank contingent usually traveled to school by the Ferry boats which crossed the river Suir in those days at fifteen minute intervals all day. Big open rowing boats, each crewed by two men. Sometimes there would be no passengers, but they faithfully maintained the each way service in all weathers. Strong men with big red hands they rowed hard against current and winds. Sometimes they would allow us to row the boats and I remember the huge oars which would nearly pull the arms away. The cost of our weekly ticket was three old pence, and for this you could take that twelve minute trip any time during the week. The ferrymen on cold wet days would be wrapped in oil cloths, and they always saw to it that we were well protected. They were full of weather lore, river lore and kindness, and they were very concerned that we would get on well at school. 'Don't waste your time now, your Mother is rearing you hard' we would be told. All the moods of that great Waterford river were known to us. The waves could be near mountainous on the day when the river would be swept with an easterly breeze, and during the late spring and all through summer it was an idyllic experience to cross that great expanse of dark green water as it lapped the quays, and looked south to the lush, tree lined banks, Cromwell's Rock and Fitzgerald's Island.

The Head Master of St. Patrick's had a fetish about punctuality, and he could not accept that our ferryboat was not a clockwork invention, but subject to all the moods of all great rivers. There were mornings, for instance, when Burton (one of the ferrymen and so named by us because he looked like a tailor's dummy in a shop of that name) would decide to tarry for a while because of a heavy swell. The Head Master would be lurking behind closed doors, and would suddenly pounce on us pale faced and angry, and take us into his office, and inflict four cruel strokes of the cane on our palms. It seemed unjust that we should have to suffer because of the mood of the river and Burton. Eventually, because of his impatience about our punctuality the small Ferrybank group went to school by bus, a decision which took some of the adventure from our schooldays.

Brother Patrick was our favourite teacher, and he treated us very seriously and affectionately, and was very generous with his tremendous store of classical knowledge. We were given the books of Jane Austin, the Brontes or George Eliott to read, and to give our opinions of them in weekly essays or reviews. He spoke lovingly of Matthew Arnold's 'Scholar Gypsy', Milton's poems and he read Shakespeare with us in a way that gave us a sense of status that we were knowledgeable. He recited Latin poems, prose and criticized our essays, and he came out then and played hurling and football with us. Our school team played Lismore and New Ross and there were many joyous days.

The examination, that dire ritual of Irish education was

always lurking in the background, threatening us all. The intercert, the leaving cert, the junior executive officers, clerical officers, local Government officers were all attempted, but few of us were successful, because there was never the cramming or the urgency of the examination test. So mercifully there were many who got through the whole school without doing any exams at all, and I believe were the better for it. By this stage, we were all interested in girls, particularly in the attractive and well proportioned young ladies attending Bishop Foy, a renowned Protestant establishment since closed. The girls usually cycled up past our school in Newtown in the late afternoon, and there were always much knees and thighs to be seen, which on a dull day were something to look forward to. The left wing of the class closest to the window was usually crowded on those afternoons. But the memory of those retreats was still vivid, and we took care, of course, not to take too much pleasure in the sight of those bare knees, or allowed those bad thoughts (which tended to obscure the text of Horace Odes, book 5) to entertain us too deeply. Still, we fell in love with the cycling girls, and began to wave to them surreptitiously. They responded with flashing smiles, and then one enterprising handsome student amongst us arranged a meeting with them in a lovely remote, famous, courting area on the banks of the Suir called the Island Lane. The arrangement was, of course, during school hours, but about half a dozen of us took the day off and availed of the opportunity to meet the girls. Waterford's first real ecumenical occasion. It was a warm, lovely afternoon, on the banks of the river. We talked, ate our sandwiches and some of us even dared to kiss the girls. The news got back to our school, there was an enquiry and the guilty ones were each given a letter to their parents. It said simply that if any such conduct occurred again, the Head Master would be compelled, albeit reluctantly, to ask us to withdraw from St. Patrick's. The letter demanded an assurance from the parents that there would be no such occurrence again. I was long practiced at the art of forgery, and I wrote back in my mother's name, giving the necessary assurance that such reprehensible conduct would never occur again. The Headmaster was entirely satisfied with my letter and my Mother was not worried.

Looking back on the school from the remove of forty years it was a happy establishment, haphazard maybe, but it succeeded in injecting us all with a great deal of curiosity about many things and bring home to us all how very little we knew about anything under the sun. It was no mean feat, at the age of sixteen, and it is a state of mind that has remained with me ever since.

However, such a schooling had disadvantages. In the Ireland of 1939, with half the world locked in war, opportunities were few, and particularly so for people whose only qualifications were a vague knowledge of Shakespeare, Gerald Manley Hopkins and Jane Austin. We were faced with a hard world of depression, when there were forty applicants for every job. To be a civil servant then, sure of money every week was very Heaven. But we had given little thought to such matters in those last years of school, and went gaily on our way, playing hurling, courting girls and educating ourselves in the ways of life, clumsily and always in the dark, where no-one would see us. We borrowed books from the library, and went to see 'Gone with the Wind' and thought it was a great big sexy film. We borrowed money for dances and were awkward on the dance floor. We drank bottles of stout and hated the taste, but it was part of growing up.

CHAPTER EIGHT

The knocker rapped hard and sharp, and the staccato noise went through the silent little house. I lay in bed and listened carelessly to the impatient sounds. It was the rent man on his Monday morning rounds of collecting ten shillings from each house. He was a sharp, pale faced and sallow man, dressed in correct dark grey suit, and he never spoke to anybody. He clearly regarded himself as a man apart, tiny, brisk and efficient. This morning he seemed very insistent and he continued to bang the knocker, although obviously it was not going to be opened. His insistent knocking in front of the whole neighbourhood was meant as a kind of public chastisement, to show the neighbours that the Foleys were not paying the rent. I turned over in bed and decided that the little man could knock until doomsday. There would be no answer this morning. Anyway, there was no point. My Mother was out on purpose, in order to avoid him, because she did not have the rent to pay. That same rent of ten shillings was an enormous sum in the thirties in Ireland, and, indeed, was regarded as oppressive by some people who had left the house earlier on.

Finally I heard the patter of the rent man's little feet as he departed briskly from the six steps that led to our hall door. He was soon knocking next door, but there would be no trouble there for the Father was a Civil Servant. A few minutes later, however, another loud banging on our door that I thought would take the hinges off. Who could that be? I looked furtively out of the top window and saw the tousled and rough figure of our potato man, and he looked aggressive too. He was a kindly man who always left my

Mother in a sack of potatoes every month, and they would agree on a figure later. I would like to have given him the five bob that was his due, but as there was not a single penny in the house, it was impossible. I felt vaguely resentful that my Mother had left me to face this barrage, although of course I had not faced it.

Finally, I persuaded myself out of bed and put my clothes on. It was about 11 a.m. and I would be just in time to sign on at the local Labour Exchange. I heard my Mother humming as she came up the steps and opened the hall door. I immediately told her of the unwanted visitors. She kept on humming to herself, and told me there was a cup of tea here for me. I came downstairs and again the smallness of our little house depressed me, particularly the bare boards which seemed to accentuate the smallness of the area. My Mother had been to town and she produced a pound of butter from a bag and put some bread on the table. She never failed to produce goodies from that bag, and goodness knows now she did it, but she never left us hungry. Ard Mhuire, as the estate in which we now lived was called, was built by the Waterford Corporation, but nevertheless, within the estate, one saw the first glimmerings of a middle class emerging in Ferrybank. It was clearly a cut above the old street. The knockers were shining, the curtains trim, and prams stood outside every house. The mini revolution which had taken place was best symbolized by the fact that one married daughter of an old family in the village actually had a maid in Ard Mhuire. A fact which amazed everybody. She conducted interviews to hire the same maid, and one of the applicants was a girl from the old village. She asked her questions like – 'Can you wash baby?', 'Can you clean silver?' and 'Can you lay the table?' Later in the evening, when the applicant for the job told her Mother of the interview, the outraged parent marched up to the house of the woman who wanted the maid and conducted a loud tirade of abuse based on the interview, asking where she had got the silver. It was a trivial incident, but it does ring home the essential tribal character of the old village. But things were changing.

On my way to the Labour Exchange I saw twenty men playing pitch and toss at the street corner. All unemployed, of course, and as I crossed Redmond Bridge there were more groups of men leaning idly on the railings, whom I recognized as being kindred unemployed spirits. We nodded to each other, they knew my destination. Outside the Labour Exchange was a fifty yard queue which I thought I had avoided by coming late. Our tattered army shuffled on until finally we were inside the Exchange and in front of the grill. The clerk told me in officious tones that I had left it somewhat late. He passed me my card and I signed D.F. in the allotted space. Two days more to go before I got my ten shillings and sixpence and a voucher for a pound of beef.

It was then the clerk told me there was a job for me. I asked him eagerly what it was and he told me that there was a job collecting for the Blind Association of Ireland. Would I be in the Granville Hotel the following day at 10 a.m.? I was, and so began my first working day. An official introduced me to a young man who was blind. The job was to take him into all the business houses along the quay. He would ask for contributions and I would record the amounts. I would take him into the shop and introduce him to the Boss. Then he would make his speech. For two whole days, that seemed like eternity, I did this job. My companion was a pleasant person who must have loathed his task as much as I did. Those unctuous little sermons from the shop keepers about the value of eyesight, and then the waiting until they finally found sixpence in a corner of their waistcoat pocket. No human beings, I thought, should be subject to such indignity. On many occasions, during those two days, I was severely tempted to throw the collection box in the face of the contributors. I got £2 for my work and I told the Labour Exchange clerk the following day that the job was unsuitable. He never offered me another, and even since I have been a firm advocate of the Welfare State.

My next job was joyful. A temporary postman in high summer. I would recommend it to anybody. The route was a rural twenty mile cycle run, bicycle provided, which took me to all the twisting, leafy by-roads of Slieve Rue down to the river Barrow at Ballinlaw Ferry, a vast expanse of water, where fishermen fished in cots, and lived off the river. Lovely, innocent people who always welcomed the postman with a cup of tea in the morning. For the first two days I had an old postman as my guide, but he rarely spoke to me anyway. All his quiet chat was reserved for the customers. For two months I was the Slieve Rue postman, and I can never remember that it rained at all. It was an idyllic job, cycling up the sleepy Waterford Quay in the early morning with the sun dancing on the river, all the little boats still and silent, smoke beginning to rise from the odd chimney. My first call was at the old school house, our old family home, which made me lonely that first morning. By a long tradition the postman was given breakfast in Belmont Monastery. The breakfast was served by a monk in the reception room on a silver tray, and was a sumptuous affair. Two fried eggs, rashers, sausages, tea and toast. I remember the courtesy of the Monks and the great respect with which they treated the postman. It was a glimpse of old style monasticism, when the monasteries were the center of the whole community. Everywhere one had to convey the news of the day, and sometimes to discuss whether or not Kilkenny would win that year's All Ireland.

One knew, too, the letters which were awaited with great urgency. Those with the English postmarks. Mothers or wives would watch all day for the post for that letter on Monday. The year, remember, was 1940, and all over Ireland these letters from England had become an essential part of the home economy. 'Did you hear from Johnny?' 'No, not a shilling for two weeks'.

One felt pleased delivering those English letters with their good news. 'God bless you, postman,' was really meant. One day I misplaced a letter and did not discover it until late afternoon. I retraced my steps and cycled back five miles to deliver it. The look of intense relief on that poor woman's face lightened the journey back. The cycling rural postman is now rare, and I, luckily, did not experience the cold and wet of winter mornings, of which the old postman reminded me, when I spoke ecstatically of the rural delights. However, those two months remain as a good memory, and I never see a monk without thinking of a good breakfast.

Six weeks of idleness again, and the utter hopelessness of life on the dole before another job turned up. This time in a flour mill unloading 20 stone sacks of wheat, and all night work from midnight to 8 a.m. The lorries arrived regularly at thirty minute intervals throughout the night and then we would carry them from the lorry and pile them up to the roof in the zinc shed. The first morning when I got home I ached in every bone. It was the first time I had every experienced total exhaustion, and each morning as I walked home, this was my condition. The pay of £2. 15s.

was never earned under harder conditions.

We had one break during the night to eat our sandwiches and drink our tea. It was a never to be forgotten delight, that small respite and blessed food. The warm comradeship of my workmates who were all much older and more experienced than I, was also great. They showed me how to get the bag properly on my back, and how to use all your strength with economy of effort. They were big strong men, very patient with my inexperience. Shared hardship can be as cementing between people as shared joy. This is why working class solidarity can be disconcerting to people who have never worked on the job. Tom, a man with the biggest hands I have ever seen, was my particular companion, and his reminiscences were always alive with imagery and humour. He had worked as a navvy in all parts of England, and he never invested this activity with any romance. 'Hard work does you physical harm – I've seen the strongest men broken in health because of carrying bags or carrying the hod. Get out of it as soon as you can,' he told me in his friendly way. He told also of his great love for his wife and his many amours in England. He had a fetish for blue photographs, which he carried carefully in his wallet. 'I always bring the wallet to work, in case the wife might see it,' he said. Wives, he felt, were meant to be pure and holy and not to know about such things. It is a belief that is not uncommon even in these days of women's lib.

When the wheat harvest was stored away our jobs ended, and we all joined the dole queues again, and lined up dutifully every morning and signed our initials on our cards to show that we had no jobs. It seemed an ironic exercise in cynicism, to make us sign a card every morning in order to convince ourselves that there was no work.

But this was war time or emergency Ireland, and these memories are simply recalled to convey some of the atmosphere of hopelessness which existed among many young people and old. The problem was eventually solved by the safety valve of emigration. In the circumstances there was possibly no alternative to the dole queues and pittance which people got. Young teenagers were in the same predicament unless they joined the Army, a boring, soul-less alternative in the view of many of us. I had joined the Maritime Inscription, a voluntary naval defence force, which had the advantage of an attractive uniform, including a navy overcoat which could be used at all times, and which the girls were said to find becoming. There was no pay for a part time navy man, and the penury was becoming extremely acute. As a result all social activities were at a standstill at personal level.

I finally landed a job again as a railway labourer for eighteen months. The railway has a camaraderie all its own and then there was still that pride of 'being on the railway'. As temporary labourers we were not conscious of this, but the men in uniform were, and the various grades, porter, checker, signalman, or on the locomotive side, cleaner, fireman and driver had very real meaning for a railway man. They had been for years, the aristocrats of the working class, in well paid and pensionable jobs. The driver and his fireman, coming off the train of an afternoon with their wicker baskets, were village institutions, highly respected men of great authority. Some of that pleasant atmosphere and security was still part of railway life in the early forties, although our jobs as temporary labourers were very hard indeed. I cannot think of any harder job than to unload a lorry of leather bales, sharp as knives, tied with rough ropes, into a railway wagon. It was a job that tore the hands and every ounce of your strength away, and indeed, offered very little satisfaction, when it was completed. There are still men, God help them, who have done little else all their lives. So the next time you grumble about C.I.E. fares think of the men who load the leather wagons or who scrub out the cattle wagons at the crack of dawn or a cold winter morning with the East wind cutting along the cattle bank.

Thirty years later, as I look back on that period of my working life in Waterford, it seems like a macabre adventure. But it was the adventure of very many people in Ireland in the early thirties, and still is in the seventies. It is the reality of the basic labourer doing the toughest job for the least money. The people on whom society depends in fact. I took the emigrant boat rather than endure it.

CHAPTER NINE

Gaelic football, the other major official Irish game to us was a bastard version of mixed up soccer and rugby. Soccer was basically a Waterford game, played on the back streets of that city by barefoot boys who used rubber balls. There was a professional soccer team which played in Kilcohan Park, but we never went there, although the names of the soccer heroes, Tim O'Keeffe, Tom Arrigan and Fatty Phelan were known to us. Sometimes when we had no hurleys we played soccer ourselves, but never with any dedication or skill. Rugby was an upper class game for snobs, played by bank clerks, the boys of Waterpark, a fee paying Christian Brothers School, which had black and red uniforms, and local protestant establishments, of which there were two, Bishop Foy and Newtown School.

No, our game was hurling, and for this game we reserved all our time and skill and vigour, as boys and well into manhood. Indeed, there was no other game as far as we were concerned, and it was through hurling in those years, that we got our greatest means of self expression, both individually and as a community. It seemed to give us a self respect that was denied to us by poverty and economic deprivation. We played that game as naturally as we walked the roads. Other sports were merely games or pastimes. Hurling was different, and a way of life.

This attitude to the game was due more than anything to my Father. He taught hurling with the same enthusiasm as he imparted knowledge of every subject; he conveyed the joy of sharing a precious secret. In Ferrybank, as I have noted before, hurling was an essential part of school life.

We left our hurleys in a pile in a corner of the school hall as we arrived in the morning, and as classes ended, we dashed to get hold of them again.

My Father had been a renowned hurler, and indeed was never conscious of any other game. I remember once, when there was an international hockey game played at Christendom, an oddly named townsland of Ferrybank, how deeply surprised and delighted he was when, coming away from the game, he met a man who spoke Irish to him because he was wearing the fainne. Afterwards, he always thought of hockey as a kind of breakaway hurling, like rugby league from rugby union. The fact that hurling was an Irish game, however, was not the point at all in Ferrybank. It was the only game we knew and enjoyed, and through it we had built a tradition of which we were proud. The Gaelic Athletic Association gave practical expression to that tradition.

It was in the G.AA. club (pronounced Gee ah ah) that we first learned about conventional politics. We learned how to propose a motion or second it, about agendas, committees and all the other formulae of democratic politics. The first big political issue in the G.A.A. for us was whether the village of Ferrybank was a part of Kilkenny or Waterford for G.A.A. purposes. It became a kind of Polish Corridor situation. The river Suir which divides Ferrybank and Waterford seemed a natural border, and it was recognized as such by the Church. Ferrybank was and is part of Slieverue Parish and the Diocese of Ossory, but the village itself is within the city boundary of Waterford, although the other half of the Parish is in the County of Kilkenny for administrative purposes.

Ferrybank was something of a shuttlecock in G.A.A. matters. In the early part of the century, it had been deemed to be part of Waterford. Then later it was transferred to Kilkenny. In 1934 the G.A.A. Congress settled the question finally, and Ferrybank was transferred back to Waterford. But before taking that decision the views of the Ferrybank Club had to be obtained. The meeting held in the old School at which the decision was taken was an exciting, passionate occasion. About a hundred club members met to discuss this vital question, which was deemed to be one of allegiance. The walls in the big room of the School were hung with pictures of Ferrybank hurling teams, and it was in this room that many thorny questions were hotly debated. It was in this same school room that all had attended as boys.

The ties of admiration and affection with Kilkenny were very strong. Already the village had two All-Ireland players in Dick Morrissey of the great Kilkenny 1931 team, and Locky Byrne who played with Kilkenny All-Ireland teams of '33, '35 and '36 and Waterford '38. The older men, like my Father, had played for Waterford, but his allegiance was really to Kilkenny. His Mother was a Brennan from Tullaroan, one of the great G.A.A. families of that most famous Kilkenny hurling parish. The pro-Waterford lobby was strong, however, and they had organised their support. Men spoke and said that the village should throw in its lot with the weaker county, for the merits of the Ferrybank players would be better recognized. There were outbursts too about Kilkenny hurling, and talk that the village should retain its independence from the city which, like a big brother, would eventually swallow it up. My Father, who was chairman, had great difficulty in keeping order and retaining his own impartially. Finally, he called for a vote, and the vote was taken in deep silence, as the opposing sides lined up on opposite sides of the room. The Waterford side had scored a narrow win which, as it turned out, was probably the best decision that could be taken. There was no applause, no crowing of one side over the over. But there was great sadness in some hearts that evening, a sense that we had turned out back on home.

The first great hurling win of which I was part was in the South Kilkenny Schools Hurling League of 1937. We played as the united parish of Slieverue, and beat all the great Kilkenny strongholds, Mooncoin, Mullinavat, Kilmacow and finally Thomastown. The bonfires blazed that night as we returned in the bus, followed by practically all the village in every style of conveyance that existed. Many of the players in the team turned out to be great inter-county hurlers with Kilkenny and Waterford. I remember telling the news to my Father who was near his death at the time in Ferrybank. He smiled quietly. I was so excited I could hardly speak.

Dungarvan, in West Waterford, was the normal venue for County finals, and when we went there to play the Junior Final in 1943, it was a day to remember. Dan Fraher's field on the west side of the town in Shandon is one of the most famous hurling centres in Ireland. Fraher himself, an old Fenian and pioneer of the G.A.A. was an equally famous character. The field, lined with trees and within the sound of the sea and in walking distance of the Comeragh mountains is as level as a billiard table, as all good hurling fields should be. It was here that we saw Waterford's first big win over Cork in 1938. The Waterford team won by a few goals and the hero of the day was our own Locky Byrne, to whom we had been devoted since childhood. He scored three goals on that wet June Sunday with such panache and ease that he seemed that day to have discovered some magic hurling formula all his own. It was here too, on this lovely ground, that Waterford beat Kilkenny and Tipperary in other years, until it seemed that like Tulla, for the Clare men, the old Shandon ground was specially favoured by God when Waterford were playing.

On this particular day the gods seemed to be looking with favour on ourselves. The bus which had taken us to Dungarvan seated 32 but carried that day about 50 people. As well as the team there were young children who carried the jerseys, old veteran hurlers and fathers of players, all quietly excited. Some cycled the thirty miles to Dungarvan, others walked and hoped for a lift, a forlorn dream in those days as hitchhiking was most uncommon, but somehow they all got there, and when we lined out against Tourin, there was the usual roar of 'Up the Slip'. Our raggle-taggle army of faithful supporters were there.

Hurling, as all civilized Irish people know, is played with young ash sticks narrow and rounded in the handle, which gradually flattens until it widens out into a flat graded surface, with the weight at the rear of the boss. A hurley must have a good spring in the middle, and a real hurler knows that a stick must be balanced and tuned, like a good fiddle. When you meet the first ball and drive it back good and strong, as we did that day, against Tourin, you know the hurley is in tune. Our team were all in total harmony, hitting balls in the air and on the ground, with an almost gay abandon and great precision. 'The ball in running for them,' the Tourin men said ruefully. Hurling played on a dry sod, like we had that day, gives immense satisfaction, and real hurling men will talk with nostalgia of great points they scored from sixty yards, from a man running at top speed. This feat needs accuracy, timing and extreme skill. The kind of stroke that distinguishes players like Eddie Keher of Kilkenny and Christy Ring of Cork. That match was one that became part of the village history. Every stroke of the game was cheered, and when victory was finally achieved we were carried shoulder high to the dressing room.

And then back to Dungarvan, where those who could afford it had meat teas at three shillings, and the others plain teas of two shillings (bread and butter, tea and cake). There was, however, a great sense of occasion at being in another town.

'The old boro', as older people often described Dungarvan, always had for me, since passing through it as a child, on the way to Ring, the wonder of a big place. Grattan Square, which dominates the town, is perfectly proportioned, with its small shops, every one of which had a licence. When brightly painted, the Square give the town a Mediterranean atmosphere. Although there is no great fishing industry, nor is there a great dock, it is still a sea town. In the pubs they talk about the weather and in the dark corners of the same pubs there are often black-jerseyed fishermen, with sad eyes, drinking porter and saying nothing. A man might come in with a half dozen mackerel on a string, mouths gaping and eyes bulging.

In those days, when petrol was scarce and always too dear anyway, there was little contact between towns and young people were always glad to meet strangers. We made many friends with the girls of the town and were loathe to leave it. There were the usual difficulties in rounding up our motley crew of passengers for the bus home. At this stage they were sprawled all over the town. Our dockers were in pubs by the water talking about coal boats and the prospect of work. An unemployed Ferrybank painter was discovered painting an outhouse of a pub,

Wedding Party of Donal Foley and Patricia Dowling.
(L-R): Mrs. Kate Foley, (Sixth from Left): Pat Foley, Best Man,
brother of Donal.

Donal Foley at his desk in London.

Pat Foley, Sean MacReamoinn, Donal Foley, Pat MacReamoinn.

Pat, Donal and Donal's sister Mother Alphonsus in Rome.

Gile Foley, sister of Donal.

The Waterford Workers' Council – memories of a bitter strike.

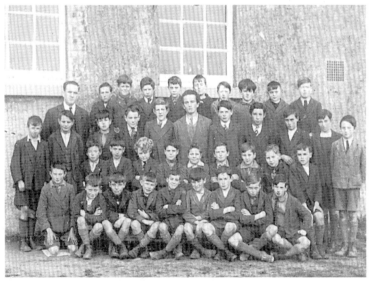

School days for Donal were surprisingly happy ones.

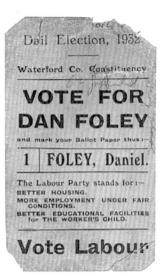

Dáil Election, 1932.

Waterford Co. Constituency

VOTE FOR
DAN FOLEY

and mark your Ballot Paper thus :—

| 1 | FOLEY, Daniel. |

The Labour Party stands for :—
BETTER HOUSING.
MORE EMPLOYMENT UNDER FAIR
CONDITIONS.
BETTER EDUCATIONAL FACILITIES
for THE WORKER'S CHILD.

Vote Labour

An early Foley family picture.
Donal on the extreme right was shortly to emigrate.

The author with Paddy Crown
(now a Garda Sergeant in
Co. Limerick).

Donal's mother who put his
Pioneer's Certificate in the bin.

It is not often realised that the author of *Man Bites Dog*, who has
made rude conversation with God comes from such a pius family.
Pictured centre Sister Maire Alphonsus, sister of the author.

Author with Donal Musgrave (extreme right, formerly a reporter with *Irish Times*), also pictured Sr. Maire Alphonsus and Brendan Foley.

man
Bites
dog
no. 6

ɒonal foley

blissfully unaware where he was and not much caring anyway. We young ones were endeavouring to 'move' our new young girl friends, and in the bus about twenty tired but happy people were sitting and singing songs.

Those outings were never totally harmonious. As some stage our supporters made contact with their rival supporters, and these contacts in the initial stages were courteous and harmonious. Mutual admiration on both sides. There was, however, always an incident, and we were always right, whatever happened. That night some of our unemployed supporters organised a draw for a packet of candles, a very scare commodity due to war time restrictions. They collected about two pounds and held a public raffle in the pub, which was won by one of our own men. The candles were duly presented, and then put quietly back where they belonged in the first place, behind the counter in the pub. The ruse was noticed by an onlooker, and certain harsh words were spoken. As the newspapers say, skuffles broke out, and one of the incidents, which I remember, is of a group of our supporters lifting the shafts of a trap in which the rival supporters were seated. The horse reared and panicked and some of the occupants were thrown out on to the road. There was no little confusion but when the Gardai came on the scene both sides seemed totally contrite and practically kissed each other goodbye. The journey home was a medley of shouting, singing and snoring, and no public house was passed without diplomatic initiatives being taken to obtain entry.

We were not unsuccessful in getting into any tavern, which in all circumstances does not seem at all surprising. But hope is never absent when an Irishman is seeking entry into a public house, and on this occasion our negotiators, for their diplomacy and tact, would have done credit to our

Foreign Service. It was dark and silent when we reached home, although when the bus arrived all the little doors opened to hear the news.

That night I arrived home, inebriated for the first time. I thought I behaved with great sobriety as I carefully put away my hurley and equipment before going in to greet my patient Mother who was waiting in the kitchen. She congratulated me on our win, asked me if I was hungry and went to prepare a meal of cold corn beef, tea and bread and butter, but before getting down to the preparation she went to the wall and took down the framed certificate from the Pioneer Total Abstinence Association which proclaimed that I was a total abstainer from alcoholic drinks, as a reparation to the Sacred Heart for sins committed against him.

She said nothing, but simply threw the picture into the dustbin. Her action was more eloquent than anything she could say. I have never regretted the loss of that certificate; neither, I feel, did my mother.

CHAPTER TEN

That day in September, 1944 when I kissed my Mother goodbye, I did so with a very heavy heart. My absence from Ireland, I vowed that day, would be of short duration. It was not to be like that. Indeed, it was fully twenty odd years before I was enabled to return to Ireland. It was really another life time.

The usual crowd of unemployed men were standing in an aimless group at the street corner and they wished me good luck almost nonchalantly. It was not an unusual event in those days when every Irish village was being stripped of its young, as was Ireland herself. We were 'going, going, going, from the valleys and the hills,' as Parnell's sister Fanny wrote of another generation a hundred years before.

I was luckier than most. At least I had a case, albeit a cardboard one, in contrast to many of my fellow emigrants who carried their few belongings tied in a newspaper. I had a pair of shoes, a reasonable coat (a Lord have mercy, as we used to call clothes inherited from dead relatives). My brother in law had died a little time previously. The other emigrants that day were, in the main, poorly dressed. A ragged, penniless army with nothing but their health and strength to hurry them on their way. No mean attributes, mind you, in those dark days when Britain needed the workers to carry the hod, and make bombs.

I called in to say goodbye to Ned Fleming, whose pub in the Lower Slip had been a kind of club for us. We played darts there, and drank little except when an Irish ship came in with a cargo of wheat from far away Canada. Then the crews, all Ferrybank men, would insist on treating us to drinks all night, and so make a great evening of their homing.

Ned, the publican was a bachelor who was a strong Republican activist. He was a small, very wealthy man, who always threw his darts in a flick away from his stomach. He also conducted a corn store which served the farmers of Sliverue and its environs. Neddy's little store was a kind of hurling cum agricultural salon, where men sat and talked and swapped stories of long ago. Ned stood here all day and sometimes they would play cards – twenty five or solo. These games were silent, serious affairs and comment was not sought from the onlookers.

That day as I was going, Ned slipped me a pound as a present and gave me the address of a man in the Elephant & Castle who had a good reputation for giving Irish working class men a bed. It was then a kind of slum area very different from today's elegance. In fact, I did call on that same man. He showed me into a big bedroom and when he put on the light in the middle of the afternoon some forty voices called out, 'put out that fucking light.' He did so promptly and assured me that they would all be going out to work shortly, and there would be a bed for me then. Things at that stage had not got that bad.

The station at Waterford as I left was crowded with young women and men with white anxious faces and parents looking even more anxious still. The young people, like myself were mostly in their twenties, all waiting to catch the 3.45 train to Dublin and emigration. Most of the men were traveling on Wimpey's vouchers en route to the building sites of England, Power Stations, Munitions Factories, roads and bomb damaged areas. Big strong men, pale and unsure, taking up their first jobs, all of them fleeing from the demoralization of unemployment, and ready to send money home to the helpless ones still left. I was seen off by Jim 'Black' Norris, so known because of the jet colour of his hair. A few months later he was killed as a rear gunner with the R.A.F. over Germany. He was our finest corner forward as a hurler.

The train to Dublin was packed with people from Waterford, county and city. At Kilkenny the platform was crowded with young people, the mothers clinging on to them loath to let them go and anxious to get the last seconds of their companionship. So it was at all little stations, until finally Kingsbridge. This was neutral Ireland. It was a silent, expectant train. Tongues sometimes unloosed slightly apprehensively about what was in store. The story of Ireland since black '47. The Globe Hotel in Talbot Street was the Mecca of the building workers. It was there they were given their destination and their work permits. I was going to London to work on the railway and didn't have to stay in the Globe. Instead I stayed in the respectable suburb of Mount Merrion Avenue with my sister Sheila and got my first glance of suburban Dublin. It was then growing fast. We all met up later on and discovered on board a ship ironically named *'Hibernia'* that we were all to do work for the British Ministry of Labour which was described on our work permits as work of 'National Importance'.

The Irish government of the day, of which Mr. de Valera was Taoiseach, had made an agreement with the British Ministry of Labour which shipped us into exile. We had to notify our place of residence in Britain, report to the police every week, and leave the country when requested to do so by the British Home Secretary. Unquestionably an odd form of neutrality, but it did ensure that our country was not continually bombed by the Germans, although, there

69

were some strange errors when the Germans bombed the North Strand in Dublin, and made a direct hit on a lonely farm house in Mount Leinster. One of de Valera's great acts of statesmanship and charity was the occasion he sent the Dublin Fire Brigade to Belfast, when that city was burning as a result of German bombers. It seems even at this remove a more important act than that much talked about cup of tea Mr. Sean Lemass, the Irish Taoiseach, enjoyed with Mr. Terence O'Neill, the Northern Ireland Prime Minister, very many years later. There was more charity and concern involved in sending the Fire Brigade to Belfast.

The British Railways ship on which we travelled was like a travelling Irish town, moving slowly and darkly across the water. Only the voices of the people, the shouts of command of the sailors and constant gurgling of the channel disturbed the eerie silence of that night. All the lights were blacked out, the first grim reminder that we were traveling to a country at war.

Down in the bar of the ship hundreds thronged round the serving hatch and the inadequate counters looking for drink. In the corridors and on the benches men and women tried to sleep and occasionally one saw mothers pushing bottles on unwilling babies. In one corner a group of Mayo men argued about Irish Neutrality. An Englishman who tried to keep his side up was told to go back to his own country, which seemed to be just what the little man had in his mind.

For myself, I was totally confused. I did not want to leave Ireland at all. Indeed, I still did not believe I was doing so. This was a nightmare adventure in which I was involved with all these strange people and strange faces. Inside me a resentment was building up against I knew not what. Why should I have to go and leave all those others at home in comfort? I would soon go back, I told myself.

In the darkness a young clear singing Cork voice pierced the silence like a rapier: 'Boys like Barry are not cowards . . . . . British soldiers tortured Barry just because he would not tell.' A primitive feeling of fellowship with that young defiant voice welled up in my breast. The song was taken up by hundreds and when our ship landed at Holyhead, that strange chorus filled the dark air. The Customs officials and the soldiers looked on; impassive, unaware of our sentiments, even if they did mean nothing. They checked our passports, went through our luggage, for what it was, and sent us on our way.

We shuffled off the boat, a long dark crocodile of people, walking as it were into the unknown except for those among us who had known the horrors of Camden Town, Kilburn, Birmingham, Glasgow, Coventry, Leeds, Reading and Slough before now. Horrors, yes, but warm with consolations too. The welcoming pubs, the weekly wage packet and the comradeship of adversity. The muted lights showed us the general direction of the train for London and as we shuffled a dread sound, which we were later to know well as the air raid siren, reminded us that the German bombers were in the vicinity. The real meaning of those sirens only came home to me some weeks later when two Irish girls who served behind a bar were blown to their deaths.

That night we were conscious only of the sharp wind, the dark and the dreariness of Holyhead, surely the unfriendliest spot during those years in the whole world. The train stopped at Crewe first, a dark jungle of a junction with only the hissing of the steam trains, and the incomprehensible shoutings of the porters to be heard.

Cups of tea could be got if one were quick and adventurous enough to dash across two platforms. I sat tight, afraid I would get lost if I ventured away from the London train. Stations with hissing trains have always had the effect of filling me with panic, and that night was no exception. Suddenly, an authoritative cockney voice could be heard above the din. 'All chinge.' We obeyed and piled urgently on to the dark forbidding platform, clinging to our bits of luggage. In a short while the first glimmerings of grey dawn were beginning to show.

Crew looked even worse in the half light than in the stygian darkness. Women pushed laden barrows, and were continually blowing whistles. It was another reminder that Britain was at war and that women were doing the jobs normally done by men. The tearoom advertised bacon and eggs. The egg seemed to be a dark coloured black platter with a foul taste, and the rasher a slice of spam of similar hue. I protested that both tasted badly, but the young girl in charge, a smiling Wicklow girl, saw that I was an innocent. 'There will be no more fresh Irish eggs for a while', she said gaily. She explained to me that the bacon was spam from America and the eggs made of powder. 'You'll get used to it' she said, 'and even like it.' The tea was good and the bread better than we had had at home. There was a three hours unexplained wait before we eventually boarded the train for London. We seemed to be coming into London for hours. A back door view of that great city, the washing hanging out and the women cleaning the windows. We were tired, hungry and a little frightened. I had to get to Broad Street, which is in the heart of the City proper.

There is a special confusing urgency about early morning London. The people seem to be filled with a dogged determination to get somewhere fast. The heart of the City could be described as sound, even if the body was falling apart. I had never experienced a big city before, at peace or at war. Even to this day I tend to lose my way constantly in the city of Dublin. An English friend whom I had volunteered to take from Westmoreland Street to the Wicklow Hotel got lost with me, and later sent me a map of Dublin.

Euston Station, that morning seemed to be stretching itself from its slumber. People setting up their wares. Unaccustomed noise of machinery everywhere. Another scream from an air raid and the reason was all too plain. A small object like a plane was careering across the London sky, a small plane shooting out in front. 'It's all right, the engine is still going well', said a reassuring voice, a veteran of the doodle bugs, those terrible last fling weapons of Hitler. A group of us watched it in awesome fascination as it sped across the morning sky, until the engine stopped and it shot down into some unsuspecting London suburb.

I thought how extraordinary self-preservation becomes the normal behaviour. We hardly gave a fleeting thought to that sleeping London group of houses which just had had its visitor of death. Houses felled, people killed and lying in agony in the debris. I made my way to Broad Street with the help of a map which had the route etched in red pencil. I took four different buses before finally getting a No. 11 which dropped me at my destination. My cardboard case had the arms practically torn off me before I reached the Headquarters of the London, Midland & Scottish Railway to which I was to devote my talents. Old railway men call it simply the L.M.S. I was sent to Brompton and Fulham Depot in South West London right across the City. It was close to the Walham Green Theatre where later Tod

Slaughter was playing 'The Demon Barber of Fleet Street' to full houses. That Grand Guignol season also had a grand actress Ellen Pollock. It was my first taste of London culture.

That night I met my sister Cait in Mooney's Irish House in the Strand, then the longest bar in London. We clung to each other before leaving and cried profusely. She had to make her way to New Eltham where she was a nurse and me to a vague address in Victoria, which I found after hours of feeling my way in the darkness. My landlady was a kindly Waterford woman, so it wasn't a bad start. I had a room to myself with a view of a tiny garden, a good bed and it was only a few minutes walk to Victoria Underground. Never was warmth and sleep so welcome, and that night there were no sirens to send us to the air raid shelter, which was a part of every house. I was a real emigrant now.

CHAPTER ELEVEN

On a dark London night in 1944 when loneliness and the sheer isolation of a strange big city was eating at my heart, I wandered to Marble Arch, the famous London forum which cynics called the safety valve. But I was in search of a friendly Irish voice, and I found them in plenty at the famous Speakers' Corner where there were always Irish people ready to argue about causes mostly lost. It was pitch dark and one could only see dark groups and hear the passionate murmurs around such platforms as the Catholic Evidence Guild or the Socialist Party of Great Britain. One could hear the usual strong Kerry accent arguing with certainty about the existence of an all-caring God, a premise which I found difficult to uphold that particular night as the doodle bugs lit up the sky or the mysterious rockets would explode with a terrifying noise (one of those rockets gave me the greatest fright of the war years, when it lifted the underground train on which I was traveling from its tracks. We escaped injury but I learned later there had been a direct hit on the next station).

This particular night at Marble Arch is etched clearly on my mind. I listened to the dogmatism of the Catholic Evidence Guild men who were so sure of everything in those preVatican II days. The speakers of the Socialist Party of Great Britain, however, were no less certain of their point of view. Involuntarily, almost, a group of young Irish people, myself amongst them, found ourselves in a small singing group in the darkness. There was a strange eerie quality about us as we sang together The Rocks of Bawn, They're cutting the corn in Creeslough today, Oh

Mary this London, An Carrigdown and a dozen more songs I cannot remember. It was, of course, the shared loneliness that threw us together, and the joy of the remembered songs gave us happiness. I never sang like that before, and indeed never since, but the remembrance of that night did bring home to me the terrible loneliness which many young Irish people were suffering at that time. The songs of exile are a real part of Irish culture which should not be ignored.

The Irish in Britain were always the hewers of wood and drawers of water, and so they have remained to this day. Irish doctors there are, Irish engineers, nurses, teachers, clerks, journalists and the rest, but essentially it was to the heavy tasks of building to which the traditional Irish skills were dedicated. These same strengths and skills were recognized by the huge building concerns of Wimpeys and MacAlpines and those of their own countrymen too, the Murphys, Fitzpatricks, Gleesons, Gallaghers, McInerneys and McCarthys. The name of the Irishman was an honoured one in the public houses of the ghetto areas where employers knew what hard work was about. This was very much in evidence during the war and post-war years in Britain, when it was the derided but mobile Paddy who willingly did all the dirty jobs for clean money. They settled in the London ghettoes of Kilburn, Dagenham, Willesden, Harlesden, Hammersmith and in the cities such as Coventry, Birmingham, Manchester and Glasgow. They moved also to the most isolated sites in the island. Lonely, rocky areas like the one from which many of them came from, Connemara. Wherever there was hard work to be done, it was there you found the big red-handed Irishman, willing to work all the hours God made, once there was money to be had on a Friday. All the rules were broken willingly for them because they could work. Often they had no tax cards, no insurance stamps. In fact, there were no records at all of many of them. They were hard working, well paid slaves, exactly what Britain wanted to rebuild their devastated country.

London, then and now, was a series of villages and the Irish made their own of many of them. They had their own public houses, their own bookies' runners and lodging houses. They went to the same churches as much for social reasons as for some vague kind of national religious loyalty. They normally followed the local soccer team like Chelsea and retained the Irish habit of remaining on in the adjacent pubs near the grounds.

The cockneys and the Irish normally got on well together. Maybe because they didn't understand each other too well. The Irish were generous to an extraordinary degree and the cockneys seemed to have no loyalty to such things as country and tradition. King and country to them was a kind of vague boss. This all suited the ordinary Irish worker perfectly, who in general felt that Britain was a place to be looted or plundered, so long as he did his work. He did not, in fact, give the matter much thought at all. Drink, gambling and the odd trip home were his main interests. Once, I remember an Irish landlord complaining to me about his Irish lodgers. He had been bombed out and when he put in his claim for bomb damage, it was only to find that all his Irish lodgers had beaten him to it and claimed for furniture and gold watches, although they owned nothing at all in the house, which was furnished accommodation.

Another friend of mine, a sub-contractor, was found driving the same load of sand all day through a check-point, and he was paid each time he passed the point. He was eventually caught out when he was some thousand pounds richer, and sent to jail. He used to refer philosophically to the episode afterwards; 'I paid my debt to society'. His friends saw the logic of it, and only felt sorry that he had been caught at all. In those closing war years when I knew them, many of the Irish work force regarded themselves as a race apart. The British they regarded as pleasant and decent, but dull. The Irish were regarded by the British as hard working, different and totally mad, rather then dull. These were accepted fundamentals.

The disregard which the Irish felt for official rules is illustrated perhaps by the following story. A young Mayo man arrived in our digs with no work permit, a vital necessity in those days. It presented no problem for this young man who had dragged himself up by his own boot laces. He found out the address of the local labour exchange, discovered where the staff drank at lunch time. He went along the following day, listened carefully until he heard and Irish accent and insinuated himself into the company. He found out that the young man with the Irish accent was a clerk in the Employment Exchange.

Later that night he had acquired a work permit, which he showed us in the digs. A friend of the same Mayo man heard there were good jobs in a certain engineering firm. His own engineering qualification was an elementary certificate which he had acquired at the age of 13 at the local tech. It was all printed in Irish, but when he presented it together with a micrometer, a most complicated engineering instrument which he had borrowed, he had no difficulty in getting a responsible post in the same engineering works on the grounds he was a highly skilled man. He held the job for at least twelve months, and only lost it when he tried to introduce a new productivity scheme. Such was the spirit of adventure that animated many Irishmen in those years, and the great success stories of the Irish can be traced in many instances to this attitude.

Of course, this is not the whole story. There were the misfits, the prostitutes who used to wear the shamrock along Piccadilly on St. Patrick's day, the winos waiting outside the pubs in the Edgeware Road, and the young Irishmen who filled the hostels for down and outs. Hopeless young Irish people of both sexes who just could not cope and had been driven into exile by desperation or very often an unwanted pregnancy.

The trains arriving at Euston in the immediate post war years were often filled with Irish people, penniless and with no place to go, who threw themselves on the welfare services of the great impersonal world of Britain. Very often they received the warmth and affection which was denied to them at home. In my experience Irish doctors and graduates quickly assumed membership of the British middle class, because, in the words of some cynical Irishman of those years 'they did not want to know'.

Those Irish people who were determined to hold on to their Irishness in the cultural sense were few, but are still recalled for their steadfastness to something that they were not at all clear about. 'Being Irish' was not a term that was exactly defined for anybody.

In 1944 and throughout the previous war years, classes in Irish were held regularly. There was an obscure room in Hammersmith up about six flights of stairs where Irish people used to foregather to dance ceili and talk to each other in halting Irish. The London County Council in fact organised many such classes and they were well attended. At many centers in Britain during the worst years of the air raids Irish people were meeting to learn the Irish language and the intricate steps of the High Caul Cap and the Sixteen Hand Reel in meticulous fashion. Many were of the extreme purist variety, and would refer scathingly to ceili and the old time waltzing as 'mixed rackets' in an Irish cockney accent.

Shortly after my arrival in London I met my future wife and we went to a ceili in Clapham Common. This was held in a basement hall, and the same night was a particularly bad one in the history of London. The terrorsome rockets had arrived on the scene, but this did not deter the enthusiasm of the dancers. The Irish dances were performed with all the care of a Mansion House Gaelic League ceili of the thirties. During a respite, an old stalwart Irish nationalist was persuaded to give a recitation. His choice was 'May God's curse be on you, England', as if the creator was not already doing his anti-British bit that night. He was received with a certain muted enthusiasm but he still insisted on an encore. Owen Roe's lament 'May God wither up their hearts, may their blood cease to flow, May they walk in living death, who poisoned Owen Roe.'

The man was a typical gentle nationalist, who would most certainly not approve of the I.R.A. today. He was know to his intimates as 'Pikestaff' because when he married his friends presented him with a Pike, the weapon used by the Irish in the 1798 rebellion.

CHAPTER TWELVE

A great many of the pubs in Britain are managed by Irishmen or their descendants and they have maintained a tradition of their own. It was to these pubs in London that the Irish people would finally drift. Typical of such institutions was Paddy Whitty's in Victoria, The Lord High Admiral, a large undistinguished three roomed pub, where the landlord, Paddy, a renowned Kerry footballer presided, with warmth and affection towards his motley crew of customers, who were mostly Irish, but well leavened with a sprinkling of cockney workers. The atmosphere, however, was unmistakenly Irish and provincial.

These Irish pubs served as community centers where the rootless Irish immigrants met and were mostly likely to meet someone from home. It seemed to be essential for these Irish people to maintain a strong sense of identity with their home places in Ireland. They followed the fortunes of the local county team, or indeed, the village with far greater intensity than the people at home in Ireland. A person who, if he were at home in Kerry or Cork would hardly cross the road to look at a match, became an aggressive fan when in Britain. It was, in a sense, a reaction against the anonymity of the big city. In the pubs, the foibles of the Irishman often became more apparent, for instance he liked it to be known, both to his Irish and English friends, that he had a good knowledge of horse racing and, more important, that he was intimate with trainers and jockeys.

Saturday mornings, it was normal for Irishmen to assemble in these Irish pubs and exchange information about horse racing. The pubs were more reminiscent of bookmakers' shops than publicans'. The publicans usually acted as bookmakers, because there were no licensed shops.

A man would arrive from Ireland, back from his holidays, and announce casually that he had been drinking with Paddy Prendergast, the famous Irish racing trainer, the previous night. Paddy, he would tell the Governor of the pub confidentially, said that so and so horse 'would be trying.' This was the kind of jargon understatement used to convey the information that the particular horse in racing parlance, was 'on the job.' The news, straight from the horse's mouth, would spread throughout the pub in some invisible manner, until eventually everybody was aware of the tip. Men calling for pints would mutter the horse's name through the sides of their mouths. There were urgent confidential consultations with the publican, and the name of the horse would be written down on a piece of paper and given to the Governor with fistfuls of pound notes. If the animal won the joy would be unconfined, and the man who conveyed the information toasted on all sides. Clearly he was in the know, and the magic circle of Paddy Prendergast.

On the other hand, if the horse was unsuccessful, although there would be no downright condemnation, the informant would in future be treated with reservation at least. The giving of tips, and the whole business of horse racing was a serious matter and it was no place for amateurs. The dogs, of course, was another story altogether. White City, Stamford Bridge, Wembley, Wimbledon and the many other dog racing tracks in London were always much frequented by the Irish, and the racing times of greyhounds were a normal part of pub conversation. These were statistics that were essential before one dared to take part in talk about the dogs. Many Irish labourers achieved their ambition of owning their own greyhounds. Others were successful as trainers and indeed, not a few tracks had Irishmen in top administrative positions. It was essentially a working class sport, and one in which the Irish felt very much at home.

At Christmas time and at summer holidays, the pub talk normally turned to sailing tickets. These were the tickets which were essential before one bought a rail ticket for the long dreary journey to Ireland. The man who could get a sailing ticket had a status all of his own. It was a simple process to write away to British Railways in time, in order to get a ticket. But simplicity was never the way of the Irish. One always talked to a man, who specialized in getting bundles of tickets in advance, and so these men gained a reputation all of their own, for this strange ability.

The G.A.A. bank holiday games in London were, in fact great festive occasions, and the pubs around Mitcham, Wembley and New Eltham benefited greatly from these Irish outings. Fathers took their children to let them see hurling and football played for the first time. The players from such strongholds as Kilkenny, Cork and Tipperary always seemed to give something extra. Proud parents would introduce them to their children, and the players seemed to be moved to much kindnesses on such occasions, and often would part with their hurleys as presents.

At first the British press jeered at the Irish games, and produced silly false reports for their English readers about Mary and Bridget screaming at the players from the sidelines, and the players themselves behaving like half tamed animals. It was a throwback to the stage Irish days, and the Fleet Street press felt that Gaelic games were simply an extension of the pigs in the kitchen syndrome. This phase which went on for many years has now ended, and the games are reported in straight forward fashion. Television cameras played their own role in this change of attitude. It was difficult for Fleet Street to conjure up picturesque, bizarre stories of the games when people actually saw them on their own screens. The British papers now produce supplements on the G.A.A. matches, a recognition perhaps from the hard headed men of Fleet Street that the Irish games in Britain have a large following.

Politically the Irish in post war years made little impact on the British scene, and as a result attempts to make the question of partition an issue in British politics failed dismally. When anti-partition candidates were put forward they lost their deposits, and failed to gain the support of the ordinary Irish worker. It was understandable, because traditionally the Irish gave their allegiance to the Labour Party. The new immigrants of the war and post-war years although not as politically conscious as their predecessors, nevertheless had vague sympathies with labour aspirations, and were instinctively suspicious of the Tories. When they voted it was normally the Labour Party which benefited.

The traditional Irish adherence to the labour cause was explained by Clement Attlee, the Prime Minister in the 1945 Labour Government, in his book, *'The Labour Party in Perspective'*. He paid a tribute to the role of the Irish in the beginning of the century in building up the young Labour movement. He attributed their efforts to the fact that the Irish came to Britain imbued with the spirit of revolution from a country which at that time was oppressed. The Irish had been coming in this manner throughout the second half of the 19th century. It was natural that they should associate with the party of the weak and oppressed in Britain. In the docklands area of London, all solid labour boroughs, and rich in Irish allegiance, there is much evidence of the early devotion of those early settlers to trade unionism and labour.

I recall one night in the fifties, in the borough of Stepney in the East End of London, when two Irish women, then in their seventies, Mrs. Long and Mrs. Alyward were made the first Freemen of the Borough of Stepney. The third Freeman was Clement Attlee himself. The two Irish women had both been Mayors of the Borough, so had their sons. The women had emigrated with their families from Ireland. This tradition of the Irish giving their support to Labour in the working class boroughs of London still persists.

They have also held strongly to their religious faith. The huge Corpus Christi processions, with all their colour and pageantry are a feature of Irish Catholic life in East London. In the old days these processions were as much national demonstrations as religious in character. The Irish bands, the famous Borough Pipers, for instance, were very much a part of this East End culture, and although big changes have taken place in the intervening years, the relationship with Ireland still continues. The last great Irish demonstration in the East End was when the funeral of Terence MacSweeney, the Irish patriot, took place from Southwark Cathedral in 1920. He had undergone a fast of seventy days. This kind of aggressive allegiance and Irish political activity which was progressive, is now minimal. The great Irish political movements which swept Britain during the days of the Irish national struggle, such as the Irish Self-Determination League are now a memory only talked about when old Irish men meet.

The last big attempt to mould the Irish into a political grouping on Irish national questions took place in the early forties and fifties, following the passing of the Ireland Act. The principal clause in the Act which caused offence was that which guaranteed the constitutional position of Northern Ireland unless the Northern Ireland Government decreed otherwise. The clause only became known during a nationwide Anti-Partition tour of Britain by Eamon de Valera when he was out of office. These Anti-Partition meetings were extremely well attended. Some 6,000 Irish people in London paid an average price of 10/- to attend the de Valera Rally at the Empress Hall, Earls Court, but it was more a sentimental and emotional, rather than the beginning of a new political movement.

At that stage any hope of organizing the Irish into a mass movement in Britain was a forlorn one. The Irish in Britain were doing well, and many of their children were pursuing University courses. They were able to have their annual holidays at home or abroad, and were experiencing the benefits of the welfare state. It was in sharp contrast with their lot at home under an Irish government. They were in the main well pleased with themselves, and it was not surprising that Anti-Partition candidates lost their deposits.

In those years attempts were made to organize the Irish in Britain through County Associations, and although little success was achieved in the main, the great mass of the Irish in Britain stood aloof from Organisations. They had settled into suburbia, solid working class areas like Kilburn in London or Daganham in Essex, and many of them remained mobile, willing to work still in any part of Britain where there was money to be made in the building trade.

They were working the lump for the big contractors, and as has transpired since, did not have any insurance stamps or any other means of identification with the country in which they were working.

But they were a tiny minority. The great mass of Irish workers were, like their forefathers who came as famine immigrants, hard working and settled in their new surroundings. They did not need at all the speeches of the Irish Bishops in the forties and fifties to tell them about the influences of alien cultures and Pagan practices. In fact, the most of them resented these patronizing sermons. The Irish were standing on their own feet. Some had become Captains of Golf Clubs, others Foremen in their jobs, and very many staunch trade unionists. They were swarming in from the back streets to take their rightful place in the society which they had done so much to rebuild.

CHAPTER THIRTEEN

A job in the station was enormously boring in itself, but the liveliness of the people there, clerks, porters, guards, carters and their helpers made the place acceptable. At the station was a goods yard to which two trains a day came with groceries, clothes, kitchen utensils, confectionery and other goods which made up the stock of the shops in Fulham in Kensington. In those days the goods were constantly lost through bombings, but the shopkeepers in the neighbourhood found it extremely difficult to believe it when their particular consignment was destroyed. I found it difficult to understand their cockney accents when they rang up to complain, and they had trouble with mine, fresh from Ireland. 'Oh, for Chrissake Paddy, put on somebody who can talk English,' was a typical retort to my patient explanation that the case in question had not arrived. As my irritation grew it seemed also that my pure Irish accent became increasingly incomprehensible to the people at the other end of the line, something which genuinely amused my colleagues.

The conditions under which we worked were Dickensian. Our office was a felt roofed ramshackle room in the middle of the goods yard, where motors and horses constantly moved. The big brown wooden desks were dirty, sloping and high, and so were the backless high stools which we sat upon. The windows were dirty and small, and so we needed the old fashioned gas lights which were never out. The two doors of the office were never closed, and the temperature, therefore, was rarely above freezing point. But these conditions never seemed to worry my colleagues in the office who accepted every discomfort with a stoicism which was very much a part of London at that time. The people rarely complained even when their houses were destroyed, or their favourite pubs bombed out. It was all acceptable like the inevitability of war.

Those were the great days of steam radio, and this particular medium played a great role in everybody's lives, far greater than television does nowadays. Conversation was constantly about radio programmes, particularly I.T.M.A., the famous Tommy Handley weekly show, and Much Binding in the Marsh, which was also very popular. Tommy Handley, at that period in war time Britain, was a recognized national institution, and he succeeded by what seemed to be a series of very simple catch phrases in keeping the whole of Britain laughing at their misfortunes, in what must have been the most trying time in the country's history. Colonel Chinstrap, Miss Hotchkiss, Miss Moanalot and the other ITMA characters were part of our daily lives in that office. Outside the office the simplicity of Londoners themselves seemed to conceal a tremendously brave spirit. Every night one saw thousands of families, young and old, going to bed on the platforms of the Underground Stations. They changed into their night attire and got into their bunks, as the trains moved in and out of the stations. They were determined, and they succeeded in keeping their city moving. The stringent war time rationing did not seem to worry ordinary people. In the rough and ready canteen of the station we were provided with dishes such as sausage toad, Lancashire hotpot, a stew, a mixture mainly of vegetables, and there were always fried bread, lashings of tea, bread and margarine. To a young healthy hungry Irishman like myself it was satisfying, although strange.

The worst discomfort for me was the scarcity of beer

and also its poor watery quality when it was available, a great contrast to the Irish pints of Guinness. It was not unusual to find pubs closed on Monday with a sign pinned on the door saying 'No beer until Friday'. This meant for most Londoners that their meeting pace was not available and they would be forced to stay in their bedsitters or flats during the many alerts during those hazardous nights. For the British pub, unlike its Irish counterpart, was very much a family center.

It was good to be in London on V.E. Day (Victory Europe Day) and to savour, with Londoners themselves, the first joys of normal life. We, a group of young Irish people, celebrated in common with many thousands of Londoners, the end of the war, in a milling mass outside Buckingham Palace, when the King and Queen and Winston Churchill and his cabinet appeared on the balcony. We cheered with the rest. The people that day were delirious with relief, and total strangers hugged and kissed each other in the streets. Some people waved tiny Union Jacks to herald the new peace. But in general it was not a chauvinistic occasion. The war was over, and those blue skies above us were safe again, no more would we see those lighted flying bombs in the sky at the dead of night, the Underground Station platforms would no longer be the dormitories of London. Was it any wonder that ordinary Londoners and people from all over the world joined together to crowd the streets, the squares and the parks of the capital? It was a joyously infectious occasion, and the cockneys who had endured so much decided it was their day of days. They danced in the streets and sang Knees Up Mother Brown. They crowded in the pubs of London, drank mild and bitter and joined in the chorus of My Old Man and Knocked Them in the Old Kent Road – all the cockney favourites. Some old cockneys heard our Irish accents and called on us to sing When Irish Eyes are Smiling, which we did, and they all joined in the chorus. Then we sang them Keep the Home Fires Burning and It's a Long Way to Tipperary, until the little pub near Victoria Station was totally dry. It was a day to remember.

Some little time later I drifted from my work of National Importance on the railways to Covent Garden fruit market, that maze of streets between Charing Cross Road, the Strand and Bow Street. Incongruously, it was to this area, right in the center of the traffic of London, that the vegetables and fruit were brought from the docks for re-distribution. From dawn until late morning every day the area presented a study in chaos. It was an area throbbing with life.

Covent Garden had many attractions for me. It was part of the West End, on the fringes of theatre land, close to Fleet Street, the home of newspaper publications, an activity which always held a great interest for me. Close by also was Charing Cross Road where there were many interesting bookshops, particularly Foyles which, in those days, had a very good Irish section. I spent many an interesting lunch hour browsing through long forgotten Irish authors.

Covent Garden was a shabby, ramshackle district. In the mornings the warehouses were stacked high with hundreds of cases of fruit and vegetables, peaches from Spain, tomatoes from the Canary Islands, grapes, lemons, apples and oranges all making a lovely sweet smelling profusion. By some miracle of the porters, the fruit and vegetables would all be loaded on to waiting lorries and sent to their destinations in outlying towns of London and inlying suburbs. The manipulation of the full barrels through the crowded streets was a feat of dexterity manual and vocal. 'Hy mate, mind your plates of meat' the porters cried as they rushed the loaded barrels around. By early afternoon the market would be as quiet as a tomb.

Because they worked from very early morning the porters, who used to wear specially made hats to carry boxes, were entitled to drink at dawn, like their counterparts in the fishmarket, Billingsgate. There language was no less colourful. These small communities which work the London markets and the docks are an essential part of London life and their spirit of comradeship gives London that particular diversity which is its strength.

The market was bounded on the East by Bow Street, where there is a famous magistrates court. I often went there as a truant from my work as a clerk in the fruit merchants to watch justice dispensed daily. The court was a good barometer of London life. Prostitution was rife in the streets and everyday the Bow Street magistrate went through the ritual of fining the girls for soliciting in the West End streets. Each girl was fined once or twice a month only. It was all done very fairly by the Police, who realize that the ladies of Mrs. Warren's profession had to live also. The magistrate hardly looked up as he pronounced the ritual fine.

The homosexuals, on the other hand, were treated with unconcealed hostility by everybody. Usually they were butlers or gentlemen's gentlemen, timid little men who were often subjected to harsh abuse by the magistrate. 'Do you know what you are?' he would demand of the frail figure in the dock. 'No, sir' the man would answer. 'Well I will tell you. You are a filthy lavatory pest,' the magistrate would helpfully prompt him. He would then go to fine him the maximum amount. One day Brendan Behan was tried in Bow Street for being drunk on a street in Mayfair. In the dock that day were a number of prostitutes who gave the Irishman a warm welcome. Brendan looked sick and tousled in the court. When the magistrate said 'Is there anything known?' there was a titter in the court. Brendan proceeded to give a number of his own misdemeanors and went onto praise the Police for their kindness to him. He was fined and left the court to warm cries from the prostitutes: 'Come back soon, Brendan.' It was a promise he was not able to keep, as not long afterwards he was dead. Another famous writer, Oscar Wilde, did not fare so well at the hands of the fair ladies. They jeered and booed him and in general were hostile. It was, of course, the mood of the day, and the girls were only reflecting it. Bow Street, as I have said, was a good barometer.

CHAPTER FOURTEEN

I had always wanted to work in Fleet Street on a newspaper and never had any illusions at all about the nature of that work. It was, I know, far removed from the urbane world of writing, and writers like G. K. Chesterton, Hilaire Belloc, G.B.S. and H. G. Wells, the journalistic writing names that were still much talked about, albeit nostalgically, in Fleet Street when I took my first job there in the late forties. I got the job on the paper through continually submitting articles and news stories to the *Irish Press.* Finally, because of my persistence, I got daily casual work from the *Irish Press.* The first day there I wrote the column 'In Britain Today' because the London Editor had gone on holidays. Jim McGuinness, later Editor of the *Irish Press,* had recommended me.

It was the smelly world of printer's ink, deadlines, stories, scoops and speed with words that had always fascinated me. The men I met every day henceforth in the Street were mainly word mechanics, who never seemed to get excited about any event, and who had seen it all before. Cynical but kind men, they were direct in their speech as they were in their journalism. It was not a world of idealism, nor of creative activity, but to me, still so much more exciting and challenging than selling wholesale fruit.

Irish newspapermen were lucky, because although they worked in Fleet Street they were not part of the main stream. We did not realize it at the time, but we did not have to suffer the pressures of the village which Fleet Street was then. Nor did we have to accept the strange news values which would make the *Daily Mirror* or the *Daily Express* splash as lead story an heiress running away with a penniless labourer. The same story might not merit attention at all in the *Guardian* or the *Times*. It was a strange jungle of confused values justified in the eyes of the proprietors by increased sales. The circulation figures were the answer to every question. It was the pursuit of values like this that eventually led to the end of many popular papers. Indeed some were the better ones, like the *Star* and *News Chronicle* which had circulations of over a million. But what were these figures compared with the four or five million figures of the *Mirror* or the *Express*. The national circulation figures became in themselves destructive.

The circulation war had many odd side results. The privacy of individuals for instance was not much respected. Politicians were often subjected to the vilest campaigns, and subjected to totally unjustifiable invasion of privacy. Indeed, many journalists felt they had every right to enter any function, private or otherwise.

Anuerin Bevan, for instance, the silver tongued Welsh miner who became a brilliant and legendary Minister for Health in the Labour Government of 1945, became a particular target of the newspaper proprietors. Journalists were sent by their news editors to hold constant vigil outside his private house in Cliveden Place, Chelsea, and report on all his visitors. If some of his friends from the left wing of the party arrived for a drink at his house, it became in the newspapers the headline 'Left-wingers in Bevan Conspiracy'. If they were foreigners, it became 'International Top Secret Meeting at Bevan Home'. It is ironic to remember that when Bevan died prematurely the leader writers dipped their pens in purple ink to write eulogies for the man who had been their constant ogre.

The circulation wars between the Sunday papers were

even more intense and cynical. I remember one time when a popular British Sunday paper had a big story in their Irish edition (an important fringe circulation figure) on the Miracle at Lourdes, featuring a serialization of the Song of Bernadette. The same space in the British edition of the paper had a long exposure of Call Girls in the West End. Fleet Street was then a sordid business which was served by decent men who were corrupted by expense accounts. I remember when I did a short stint on one of the popular Sundays being sent down to the East End to the wedding of a man who had deserted the Army. The newspaper knew that the Redcaps were arriving at the celebrations and arresting the bridegroom. A picture had been arranged with the couple so that the paper had an exclusive story. I went down to the East End, was given a warm welcome by everybody, and accepted hospitality. I phoned through a few paragraphs and then accompanied the bridegroom and bride to Waterloo Station where he was taken to Aldershot Barracks. I went back to the Office and described the heart-rendering scene. The News Editor asked me to put in my expenses, but I told him that there had been none, as I had taken an office car to the East End and the Station. The decent man however pointed out to me that the story was the off-lead and therefore merited expenses.

'Did you not buy the bride's mother and father a drink?' he demanded accusingly. 'Did you not bring down the bride a present? Did you not slip the hotel porters a tip?' and so he went on until eventually a sum of £19 had been agreed. This, of course, was in Fleet Street's more prosperous days when expenses were a tax free form of salary for journalists.

The attitudes of some of the men on the Sunday papers were extraordinary. For example, when an Irish nurse married a Scottish Duke it became a huge Fleet Street saga. Some weeks later, when the nurse's sister was being married quietly in London to an ordinary Londoner, the Sunday papers decided to make it a big national story. The wedding was crowded by reporters to the consternation of the unfortunate families. When the newspaper were not admitted, they became extremely annoyed, Indeed, one reporter told me later in Fleet Street he intended describing the bride's father as a 'burly barman' in revenge. In fact, the man, I understood, was the manager of a conservative club. A gentle quiet person, in no sense a burly barman in the meaning that term was intended to convey.

By comparison, ours was a gentle world of journalism, although it is much changed nowadays. One of my first journalistic jobs was to report the funeral of James Stephens, who wrote many of the fairy stories which delighted me as a young child. I remember the joy of reading The Charwoman's Daughter or Mary Makebelieve. The Crock of Gold was another treasured memory. The funeral took place at Kingsbury Cemetery in North London on a biting cold day, and was only attended by less than a dozen people, which reflected perhaps some of the values of Irish society at that time. Among those present were the publisher Harold MacMillan, who was later to become British Prime Minister, and John Delanty, the Irish High Commissioner, who had been a close friend, as he was, indeed, of all Irish writers. It was my first contact with the famous, and I remember feeling an awesome sense of responsibility at reporting the event. When I got two of the names misspelt, this was pointed out to me very sharply by my Boss, Jim McGuinness, who later became editor of the *Irish Press* and Head of News of R.T.E. It was my first lesson in journalism. 'Get the names right. If in doubt, leave them out.'

Harold MacMillan kindly gave a few of us a lift back to Fleet Street in his car. The great man was in reminiscent mood about Irish writers whom he seemed to hold in great affection, particularly Sean O'Casey. He told us with a chuckle how his firm had given Patrick Kavanagh a retainer for many years, with the proviso that anything he wrote would be for MacMillan. Kavanagh's next work was given to another publisher. He retained no hard feelings about the matter, but simply told it as an illustration of the wayward behaviour of writers in general. When MacMillan dropped us, I remember, we all went round to the newspaper workers' club, which was then a shed at the end of a laneway in a war devastated space behind Fleet Street. It was the place to which the printers and readers of the Press went for a drink between editions, and in the long thirsty hours when the pub were closed between 3 and 5.30pm.

It was here I met for the first time Con O'Leary who, in those days, was still a renowned Irish name in London journalism. He had, in fact, been an early victim both of his own garrulousness and warmth and the pressure of newspaper work, to which he never really grew accustomed. Con at this period was a temporary reporter, paid on a daily basis on the *Irish Press,* but as a young man he had worked in the *Guardian* under C. P. Scott, had been assistant editor of C.P.'s weekly and a leader writer during the early days of the *Sunday Express.* The leaders he wrote for Lord Beaverbrook were not allowed to mention religion or politics. Con was, in fact, one of the few remaining Fleet Street characters. He told me that day that the most depressing experience that he had to endure was to listen to false stories of his own experiences from colleagues in

Fleet Street. I had heard some myself already: how he had consumed all the altar wine in a Fleet Street church when he went to communion with a huge hangover; how he broke the windows of the A.B.C. Café every year on St. Patrick's Day because Sir Hamer Greenwood of Black and Tan fame was a director of that firm.

Con was then a sad figure. He had done enough work to keep any person in comfort. He had written half a dozen well received novels, a history of the Grand National, a collection of short stories (An Exiles Bundle) thousands of articles for the literary magazines and a play for the Abbey Theatre. It was an impressive list of work for a man who was engaged always in the daily grind of Fleet Street journalism and here he was dependant on a pittance for existence. His very presence seemed a warning to young journalists of the jungle they were entering.

Con was a slightly built man, stooped, and as he is forgotten today in Ireland, it was worth recalling something about him. He always spoke in a cultured West Cork accent and his conversations were laced with memories of his college days in Cork where he was closely associated with Daniel Corkery, who had nurtured such talents as Sean O'Faolain and Frank O'Connor. During his years on the *Guardian,* he had written many of the pro-Irish leaders for that paper during the Black and Tan period, a fact of which he was very proud. He had interviewed Terence McSwiney in Brixton Jail. When on the *Guardian* he was invited by T. P. O'Connor, the famous Tay Pay, the Irish Nationalist member for the Scotland Road Division of Liverpool, to come to London as his assistant editor on T. P. Weekly, at that time a most influential literary weekly in London. It was no secret that O'Leary did most of the work for that paper. His colleagues in Fleet Street at the time had great affection for him, and his abilities were much respected. Because of my work on the *Irish News Agency,* and later in the *Irish Press,* I was most often in the company of Con O'Leary and Terry Ward, who was the London Editor of the *Irish Press.* Terry, a Derry man, a fact he rarely allowed you to forget, wrote a lively, provocative daily column in the *Irish Press* called In Britain Today, to which Con and later myself also contributed. Ward and O'Leary were inseparable friends, but at certain stages of drinking each day, they would argue heatedly over some trivial matter, and it would normally end with Ward accusing O'Leary of being in his anecdotage. He would then order him back to work. Whereupon O'Leary would retort 'C. P. Scott never spoke to me like that'. It was, however, good natured banter, for the two men were very close in spirit. They would later be found on the bus from Fleet Street to the Strand, in order to get in the last half hours drinking between 10.30 and 11 pm in Mooney's Long Bar. It was a practice to which many journalists in Fleet Street were prone in those days. The bar has gone now, but so has this particular breed of Journalist.

CHAPTER FIFTEEN

We who worked on Irish newspapers in Fleet Street were very often together because the stories which we covered had particular Irish interest for all our readers. This meant that we were close to the ethnic Irish community in Britain; we met Irish politicians who came to London from the Republic and the North, and we tended also to go to Irish areas in London such as Kilburn, Paddington, Hammersmith, Dagenham and often also to cities such as Huddersfield, Birmingham and Manchester, where there were always closely knit and long standing Irish communities. Fleet Street Irish newspaper offices offered a unique vantage point from which to observe the Irish at home and abroad. Also many Irish people who came to London and notably journalists or writers of any kind would come down to Fleet Street to meet Terry or Con whose names were well known and whose conviviality was also legendary. These occasions became celebrations and the company was always good.

Brendan Behan was an early and constant visitor to our office in The *Irish Press* in the middle of Fleet Street. He was writing an article every Saturday for the *Irish Press* and it was always a fine piece of writing. The articles have since been published in a book 'Hold Your Hour and Have Another', and they survive that serious test for any journalist. The column was a minor comedy every week; Brendan remembering all the warmth and fun of his childhood on the North side of Dublin. His Granny and her friends and their drinking escapades, the woman who was barred from Glasnevin cemetery for being always drunk when she arrived for funerals; the story of taking the

101

tinkers' ass upstairs to drink in their tenement room on a Saturday night, are all told here with humour and compassion. Nobody enjoyed these same stories more than Brendan himself. He told them to us first in the pub, before going back to write them for his Saturday article. In those days Brendan was a shy, fat, happy, shambling, untidy man whose big body would shake with laughter when he told his stories. His stories were always funny and compassionate and mostly about his own North city people. He loved to drink pints of stout, but it was noticeable that even at that stage his personality seemed to undergo a change when he drank too much, as he often did.

He would, under the influence of drink, cease to be a companion and become a performer for an audience. At this stage in the 50's Brendan was at the height of his writing powers. The Quare Fella was produced at Joan Littlewood's theatre – the Theatre Royal, Stratford – and was widely acclaimed as a masterpiece. Behan, they said, was another Irish genius of the theatre. One critic said that the role of the Irish was to revive the English theatre in every generation by bestowing on it a work of genius. Brendan had done this, in his view.

The story of Brendan Behan's short, merry life and death is well known. He succumbed to the commercial vulgarities and the personal publicity that Fleet Street bestowed on him. Like Marilyn Munroe, he became a victim of his own legend and was unable to live with the pressures which the Behan legend generated. But he gave us in Fleet Street some great hours of pleasure and he gave me a love of the City of Dublin which will never leave me.

Patrick Kavanagh, the poet, was another constant visitor to Irish newspaper offices in Fleet Street, Kavanagh was a total contrast to Brendan, sharing only a mutual love of drink and company. He was reticent and gruff and did not suffer fools gladly. His tongue was like a rapier, and he could be cruel to lesser people than himself. He was normally ill dressed in old countryman's style, shabby grey brown overcoat and suit, soiled shirt and collar, and he would ramble down Fleet Street in a proprietorial manner as if it were part of his own Monaghan village of Inishkee.

This particular night, I told him that I would buy him a drink when I had my daily chore, the London Letter, finished. He sat down and watched me impatiently typing labouriously, offering the odd word of counsel like 'why don't you cut out the leading article from *The Standard* and send it over as the London Letter? Nobody will know the difference.'

Irish newspaper offices in Fleet Street had a special place in those years in the hearts and minds of the Irish in Britain. Sunday nights, for instance, the telephones rarely stopped ringing with requests for the G.A.A. results from Ireland. Those results were read out at Irish dance halls all over Britain. We were constantly invited to Irish functions, dinners, dances, ceilís, weddings, Gaelic functions of all kinds.

In those post-war years of the 40's and 50's a great number of Irish societies were established and others which had become obsolete were revitalized. By now the biggest number of new societies were the County Associations. These Associations were born through a desire by Irish people for a particular identity in the large anonymous community of Britain. It is not an unusual development in mass communication and has long been a feature of Irish life in America. In London, in particular, practically every country in Ireland had an association representing its people. It was rarely an Irish newspaperman in Britain got a Saturday night free as a result of the growth of these associations. These Irish nights became very important for Irish people, and did not go un-noticed in Ireland with the papers, local and national carrying full reports often illustrated with pictures. The functions served to give the Irish status because the Mayor of the particular London Borough from which the greatest concentration of people came, usually was present. Very often too, Irish Government Ministers and Bishops accepted invitations to be present. The functions became great occasions for long speeches and in the case of the Bishops long sermons.

The politicians usually had the good sense to tell the people (who had been driven into exile, by the ineptitude of an Irish Government) to do their best in their new country to uphold the honour of their country by being good responsible citizens.

The Bishops in the initial stages concentrated on telling the people to watch their spiritual life in this pagan land. They succeeded on many occasions in giving the impression that the Irish who went to Britain had a frightful job in remaining Christians at all. What with all these lights and dances the temptation to go off the rails was almost insurmountable! The Bishops without knowing it perhaps were being extremely patronizing and often down right stupid. Most of those attending such functions were Irish working class people whose children were attending university and enjoying the opportunities denied to them at home. They were doing well in fact, and in no need of lectures from either ecclesiastic or politician. The bright lights and temptations of Dublin, Cork, Belfast or Limerick can be just as alluring as London as their Lordships, no doubt, have reason to know.

104

Reporting these functions became a bore because of their similarity. Each particular Association felt that their particular function was the greatest event of the year, but it became more difficult to get a paragraph for the London Letter out of them. This had become for the cynical a criterion of their importance. One such event I recall I did not attend at all, but instead drank in Fleet Street all night with a very entertaining journalist, the late 'Bud' Bassent of *The Belfast News Letter.* When the speeches were well over I arrived at the function and seeing a colleague from a rival Irish newspaper, I asked him what had been said. To my surprise, he refused to tell me and I was 'stuck' as they say in newspaper parlance. The speaker was an Irish bishop, and having heard so many I decided that I knew exactly what he would say. I phoned up my paper in Dublin with a speech taken from that productive area – the top of my head. It was given great prominence in the paper.

The speech talked about the importance of joining a trade union, equipping themselves for leadership in life by utilising the excellent adult education services available in London, and that it was essential to become part of the local community, preferably the local Parish and to get to know the Parish Priest. All excellent adherents with which no bishop dare disassociate. I met the Bishop concerned next day and apologized for not being present and confessed to him basically what I had done. He was greatly amused, complimented me on what I had done and said that it was a pity that he had not made such an excellent speech himself. The outcome was funnier still; my colleague, who had refused me the speech the night before was severely reprimanded by his News Editor who told him they had missed the whole point of the speech. I agreed with him.

There was a distinct class division among the London Irish which was very clear in their organizations and societies. The Irish Club and the National University of Ireland Club were in the eyes of the membership a class above the County Associations. The professional classes, Irish doctors and dentists who were extremely numerous rarely if ever patronized the County Association functions or even those functions which groups like the Dagenham Irish would organize. (Dagenham Irish were wholly employed in the Ford Motor Works and were a very compact prosperous community which had strong links with Cork.)

The Irish Club had its own premises in Eaton Square, a very fashionable elegant square close to the West End. The membership was largely made up of Irish white collar workers, civil servants, teachers, and a few doctors and dentists. The Club demanded a lot of attention from Irish newspapers and sometimes put on entertainments, lecturers and exhibitions. Although it boasted that it was a classless all embracing institution, it never achieved this distinction and became largely a haven for those who liked a drink and also a meeting place for Irish people on business in London. But the Irish Club did also provide a meeting place for Irish people who lived in flats and who liked to take part in a programme of Irish activities – dancing, concerts, drama and Irish language and choral classes.

The National University of Ireland Club regarded itself as slightly above the Irish Club, its members being largely doctors and dentists. Theirs was a largely exclusive operation until St. Patrick's Day when they held a Ball in Grosvenor House, one of London's top hotels in Park Lane. The Taoiseach often attended the function, together with the Cardinal Archbishop of Westminster. All the professional Irish would normally emerge from their suburban fastnesses for the occasion bedecked in Shamrock and anxious to learn from the Taoiseach's own lips about the state of the 'ould country.'

Down the road in The Hyde Park Hotel, the Irish Club held their annual St. Patrick's Dinner and this was no less fashionable or elegant, although the members of both would disagree. In more recent years the 60's British Ministers including Harold Wilson attended these functions and spoke about Irish unity – not a topic which would not trouble the diners a great deal at each function.

Still, I remember St. Patrick's Day outside Ireland with affection. In London, even the prostitutes wear their shamrock with pride, many of them perfectly entitled to do so having impeccable racial qualifications. Although St. Patrick's Day is not a bank holiday in Britain it was a holiday for the Irish who liked to assert their nationality in their own very individual way. For Irish journalists it was one of the very busy day's of the year. The news, however, was always good – St. Patrick gave us little trouble.

One of the saddest times, in retrospect, was the occasion when a mission in the Irish language was held in Huddersfield, the North of England industrial town. The mission, conducted by two Irish Redemptorist priests was, the local Catholic priests felt, necessary because the Connemara immigrants who populated St. Patrick's Parish were finding it difficult to understand sermons in English, even when spoken by Irish priests. The Connemara people, numbering a few thousand, lived protectively together in this city of Georgian houses; they used Irish normally and were known locally as 'The Connemaras'. They were hard working, mostly employed in the building business 'muck shifting' as the native English called it. They had large families and had a long standing tradition of emigration to this area and were well liked locally for their law abiding and solid citizen qualities.

A local priest took me to one of the Connemara lodging houses. Some fifteen men were sitting around a big wooden table in the big old fashioned kitchen. It was dinner time and a young attractive woman was serving them, baby in arms, with big dishes of mutton stew. When they saw us they took me to be another Irishman in search of work and began to discuss me in very idiomatic Irish but also in a very amusing sophisticated fashion. Having listened to them for sometime I eventually broke in on the talk in Irish. Silence for a moment, but then friendly, warm laughter.

Afterwards they took me to the pub where we drank heavily, sang Irish songs and came back to the house loaded down with bottles. It was a great Irish night and an insight into one of the reasons why the Gaeltacht at home was dying. There were no jobs and consequently no porter for people. Culture I learned that night is about having jobs as well as language, songs and dancing.

In fact those Connemara exiles had a problem which faces all emigrant communities. Their children were growing up English speakers, and therefore were not having the communication which they needed with their parents who still used Irish among themselves at home. It was a fact which worried the teachers and priests in that Huddersfield. It was a form of alienation that they did not want to see develop – a ghetto situation on the kitchen floor – the final irony of Irish emigration.

CHAPTER SIXTEEN

In the mid 50s I crossed Fleet Street from the *Irish Press* Office, and joined the London staff of the *Irish Times*. It was not such a decisive step as one might be led to believe, as there had always been and still is a fairly strong movement of staff between these two particular Irish newspapers. I was the only commoner, however, in British class terms, in my new office – my fellow journalists were the Hon. Michael Campbell, the younger son of Lord Glenavy and now a well known novelist, and John Arnott (the present Sir John) – whose family had a controlling interest in the paper.

The little rickety dark office on the second floor, above the cricketer Jack Hobbs' shop, in the middle of Fleet Street, close to Mooney's pub, was more of a literary salon than a newspaper office. This was made clear to me humourously on my arrival by my colleague Michael Campbell. Their main daily task was the compilation of the London Letter, a 1200 word discursive commentary on life in Britain, political, social, economic and cultural. It was, we were told, generally accepted in Ireland as a most readable and important section of the *Irish Times*, the readership in those days being very much orientated towards Britain. The London Letter did give an opportunity for comment on all sorts of happenings in Britain and for information which would not otherwise appear in the news pages. It was killed some years ago as the paper changed its emphasis and became more solidly centered on life in Ireland. Perhaps it was a mistake.

My job, however, was mainly concerned with news out of London because since the death of the *Irish News*

Agency (with which I had been connected) a little time previously, the *Irish Times* had felt the lack of a news service of Irish interest out of London. Both my colleagues felt that the provision of news from London was outside their duties, if not beneath them altogether. They were essentially they felt, commentators or observers of the London scene, and not reporters of it. For instance, when a dockers' strike took place in London, not a rare event then or now, Michael Campbell would comment ironically to John Arnott: "A day for the whip, Arnott, what!" It was a gambit that never failed. John would sit in front of his typewriter, typing at unusual speed, words pouring from him. He would scourge the dockers for their irresponsibility, selfish class interests and lack of loyalty to their fellow citizens. When his temper was really roused in this fashion it meant that the total work burden of the office was considerably reduced. On some occasions he would devote the whole London Letter to his anti-strike commentary. A day for the whips indeed.

The gathering of news in London gave me a valuable insight into the workings of the British press and very wise experience of all kinds of stories. There were important Press Conferences held daily in London, briefings by Ministers, events like crashes, the famous Christine Keeler and Stephen Ward court case, a tremendous variety which meant that life if not always exciting was never dull. Pandit Nehru, Bulganin and Kruschev, Eisenhower, Truman, de Gaulle, Tito, de Valera and even Sir Basil Brooke, later Lord Brookeborough came to London and met the Press. In the *Irish Press* days we were expected to ask, (and we always did) about the partition of Ireland. It was the period which became known later as "the sore thumb policy." The partition question was raised on every conceivable occasion, and Irish journalists felt it was their duty also to do so. Sometimes the Office armed us with a pertinent question about Ireland. Pandit Nehru being a friend of Mr. de Valera was always a good mark about the partition question. The alleged persecution in Eastern Europe was also pertinent, and Con O'Leary once asked Marshal Tito about his imprisonment of Archbishop Stepinac.

I remember myself once having to ask a composer who had defected from Czechoslovakia from which part of Ireland his grandmother came. The *Irish Press Office* in Dublin had been told that the composer's grandmother came originally from Ireland. The composer was unaware of his granny's whereabouts and the whole conference promptly dissolved in laughter. Such questions, although in line of duty, were a trying ordeal for a shy young Irishman like myself.

The most important and valid task in those days for an Irish newspaper man in London was to get hold of the big stories and dissect their importance to Ireland. This was particularly so of economic stories where Irish interests were at stake. The question of Irish butter quotas on the British market and the annual agricultural review by the British Minister for Agriculture are stories that spring to mind. But sometimes, seeking the Irish angle could be brought to ridiculous lengths. Always, film stars or visiting celebrities would be asked if they included Ireland in their itinerary, and sometimes as in the case of Marilyn Monroe, the film star, she should be asked by us if she intended to buy Irish tweed or fabrics of any kind for future wear.

The Monroe press conference was surrounded by unprecedented bureaucratic ballyhoo. All the newspapers, London and International, plus the Agencies were summoned to the Savoy Hotel on a Sunday afternoon by telegram from the high powered publicity agency handling Miss Monroe's visit. There was the strictest security at the Savoy Hotel, almost as bad as that for Marshal Tito whose visit and arrival up the Thames had closed all the twenty bridges of the London river. Some 300 journalists were seated in the Savoy's famous River Room, the scene normally of lavish bouquets and balls, to greet Marilyn Monroe. At intervals a dapper public relations man would come into the room to inform us in stentorian tones of Miss Monroe's immediate progress to the Hotel....she was now at Cheam in Surrey, at moments later at Croydon South, then Vauxhall. He came back a few moment later to announce that the film star had entered the Hotel, and then came the punch line: "She is here."

A small frail figure, with a beautiful pale face, dressed in a black silk dress with a bare midriff came in through the door as a million lights flashed. "Jaysus," says my colleague Cathal O'Shannon, now of R.T.E. "isn't she the little dote." The remark was broadcast all over the world. No matter, Marilyn was.

Frightened and worried she may have been that day at the gathering there to meet her as she sat with her husband the play-wright Arthur Miller, but she answered all the questions with the aplomb of a master publicist of acute intelligence. We were spared the ordeal of asking her whether or not she would buy Irish linen underwear by her husband indicating to her gently that she had had enough. I record the occasion because it does indicate how far the techniques of the professional publicity men had intruded on the workings of newspapers even at that stage in the 50s. Even for Marilyn Monroe's name to attract three hundred working journalists on a busy Sunday afternoon was no mean feat by the publicity men.

The *Irish Times* had recently started a tabloid newspaper on Sundays called the *Sunday Review,* and one of my jobs was to report for that newspaper. It was a hard hitting, tough little paper, but it had the misfortune to arrive on the Irish scene before Irish readers were ready for that kind of journalism. They have now developed a great appetite for it as the circulations in Ireland of the *Mirror* and *Mail* illustrate. The *Sunday World* is no less successful. Tabloid journalism with its simple use of words and persuasive information techniques may look deceptively easy, but the journalist craftsman knows that it is much more difficult to write 250 words on an event than 800. The condensation of information into a readable and informative language is the real test of a journalist. Probably, one reason why some of the best journalists in Fleet Street, Cassandra (R.I.P.) Dick Crossman (R.I.P.) Vincent Mulchrone, James Cameron, Malcolm Muggeridge, all worked in their day for the popular papers and the tabloids. The *Sunday Review* died the death like many other good newspapers, having played its own important role in opening up many aspects of Irish society that had remained strangely closed until well into the 60s. The *Review* in its day was regarded as vulgar, brash and irresponsible by many Irish journalists, not least those working on the *Irish Times*, but it is interesting that its columnists were snapped up when it closed and its techniques were widely adopted. Basically, the technique was that if you had a good story you hit the reader with it by professional use of print and clever illustration. And you were not afraid to say what you meant.

To return to London and our own den in Fleet Street. My divorce from the *London Letter* had only gone on for about three months. I soon became a part of that daily grind which took us to odd markings like the Chelsea

Flower Show (six years running) the Ideal Home Exhibition, (four years) the Motor Show (three years) August Monday on Hampstead Heath, The Easter Marches for the Campaign for Nuclear Disarmament, the barge trip up the Thames from Savoy Embankment to Hampton Court, Speakers' Corner and of course, the last but not least the coverage of the House of Commons for the *London Letter.*

Those were the days when Irish affairs could not be discussed at Westminster except on reserved days. A kind of Paddy's Day which was always regarded by M.P.s. of all hues with a certain amount of levity. Cahir Healy and Anthony Mulvey both Nationalist members would occasionally bore the House by raising the old chestnuts about discrimination and jerrymandering in Northern Ireland, but the Unionists who were so safe then, would blandly give the impression that it was they who were the wronged ones. Sometimes people like Geoffrey Bing, Hugh Delargy, Fenner Brockway, Willie Gallagher the communist and Michael Foot (dare one say it now) would force the Unionists to burn the midnight oil in the House in order to defend their chicanery. Bing, in particular, would have done his homework, and the Unionists were really scared of him. I think it was Captain Willie Orr a Unionist of deepest hue who dubbed him the "Horror from Hornchurch".

On the whole, however, it was a time when Irish affairs, north or south played little part in British politics. Irish reporters, like myself, had to dig deep for the stories and very often to draw the attention of M.P.s to matters screaming out for their attention, to suggest questions to them was commonplace. Neither Bernadette Devlin nor the exposing lenses of British television cameras had arrived on the British scene to let the British people know what was really happening in their name in Northern Ireland.

One major British newspaper story which hit Fleet Street in those days was the transport of Irish horses by ship to France. It was a story which was old. Horses had died on board and conditions on the ships were bad. The *Guardian* first covered the story in a feature article, but the *Daily Mirror* which loved popular campaigns in those days, saw it as a real circulation builder. The British love of animals, particularly cats, is even greater than their love of humans. Anyway, the *Mirror* did a brilliant exposure job, and the Irish Government was obviously badly advised of the impact of the story in Britain. It was only when there was talk of people canceling their Irish holidays and boycotting Irish goods, that the Irish Government finally moved. Sean Lemass came to London, held a Press Conference in the Embassy, and promised that the traffic would end. He was frank, and the Press liked him for it. That day at the Conference which was fairly wide-ranging, he spoke also of the difficulties involving sailing tickets to Dublin. He was of course critical of British Railways, but went on to say that these difficulties were often compounded by the behaviour of the Irish themselves. "Take Dun Laoghaire on a crowded bank holiday," he said "a man goes with his wife to return to England. They go into the boozer with the brother and the wife, stay longer than expected and miss the boat. If you multiply that incident by ten you have real trouble next day," he said. It was the kind of openness and knowledge that is always necessary.

It was rare in those days to find politicians speaking in such open fashion, saying in fact that we had our faults too.

Defensiveness is often the real barrier to understanding in these islands.

I recall another occasion when I had reason to admire the frankness of Sean Lemass. It was in Germany when he was given a State reception by the Government in Bonn. He seemed to me to be extremely embarrassed by all the protocol of the Germans, particularly inspecting their Guard of Honour outside the house of Dr. Adenauer the Prime Minster. He took the wrong path a few times and confessed he was not used to all this formality. Later, he was chatting with Dr. Adenauer at a reception given by the West German Government. We wanted to speak to him dearly to find out what had transpired at the luncheon. He saw us and apologized to the Prime Minster for a moment. "Excuse me, for a second, Dr. Adenauer," he said, "But these men are very important to me." "The Irish newspaper men. Oh yes, I understand," replied Dr. Adenauer knowingly.

The B.B.C. in those days often betrayed a crass ignorance and stupidity about Irish affairs, and reporters from both North and South took advantage of this. Once I remember, a Northern Ireland reporter who had heard the Soldier's Song played on the Wilfred Pickles' Programme "Have a Go" telephoned the B.B.C. and told them for the sake of a story, that the song was repugnant to many Northern Ireland people and should be withdrawn when the programme was repeated. The B.B.C. complied. The programme had taken place in the Irish Club in London and was a fully Irish occasion wholly attended by Irish people. Wilfred Pickles himself was livid about it. The affair made a story in the papers north and south, but those were the days as I have said, when the Irish were not making news as they are today. Perhaps they were better days. For some at least…..

CHAPTER SEVENTEEN

One day in September, 1963, I had a telephone call from the Editor of the *Irish Times,* Douglas Gageby to tell me that the Managing Director of the paper would be calling on me the following day. This was an unprecedented event and as the paper was doing badly, the *Evening Mail* and *Sunday Review* and *Radio Review* having been recently closed, I concluded that he was coming over to London to give me notice that my services would no longer be required. His journey to London, John Arnott and I both believed, was to soften the blow. We made plans that I should get a decent financial send off.

The following day I awaited Major MacDowell's visit with no enthusiasm at all and was agreeably surprised when he offered me the News Editorship of the paper. To go back to Dublin, however, was no easy decision. My roots were now twenty years deep in London and I now had a wife, and children who were all at school. We considered the matter that night and in a few days I accepted the job. Aer Lingus rather than British Rail were the carriers on this occasion. Perhaps in itself an indication of the half life time I had spent in London.

Sean Lemass was Taoiseach since 1959 and he had already made a considerable impression, particularly on young people by his down to earth practicality and constant talk of economic planning, that seemed to suggest a more business like approach to Irish affairs.

But cynically, I recalled to myself that this was the same Fianna Fáil Government that had driven us all to emigration twenty years previously. This was the administration too, which had presided over the emigration of over a million Irish people in the war years and after. Two brief interludes of Coalition Government had of course added their own dimension to emigration. But the people seemed to have forgotten that the new Taoiseach had been de Valera's economic expert throughout the whole era of Fianna Fáil. Nevertheless it was clear to everybody and to us emigrants in particular, that Ireland under Lemass was changing fast and adjusting itself to new International standards. The era of de Valera had ended so the Pundits said, and now the practical man of affairs was at the helm. There was, it seemed to me at any rate, an air of modernity which had been conspicuously lacking in the Ireland I had left. Lemass was inclined to talk less in Dev's visionary terms of factories and tractors. One felt listening to him on a few occasions that he would rather see a man in dungarees than in the bainins so beloved of Bord Fáilte. The Lemass philosophy too, of self-sufficiency, which he has projected so ably in the 30s had now given way to a policy of attracting industries from abroad. As a result some of the native rickety factories would have to go to the wall.

The Cabinet which Lemass led was younger and more attuned to his own views. Names like Charlie Haughey, Neil Blaney, Jack Lynch, George Colley, Brian Lenihan were being heard more and more, and the old tried and trusted old guard of Fianna Fáil who had served since 1932 were one by one either passing on or handing in their Ministerial portfolios. It was as if the holes in the shroud in which de Valera had often enveloped his chicks were beginning to let in the light. The mohair suits, expense accounts, the Mercedes cars, the packed lounge bars and dining rooms of the expensive Dublin hotels were now commonplace in the country. One welcomed this wave of prosperity, and the boom which Ireland was obviously experiencing. Still, there was a feeling of unease. Emigration continued, albeit much lighter, and the unemployment rate was still far too high. Dev was now in the Park as President, but the vision of his Ireland seemed to have gone too in the new Fianna Fáil deal.

We had gone far away from de Valera's island of young men and comely maidens rearing healthy families in Ireland, and pursuing all the traditional sports of the country side, or so it seemed at any rate. But oddly enough, side by side with the economic boom there was a deepening of interest among young people in the traditional cultural values. Traditional music and ballads and the language itself were attracting and exciting many young people in Ireland.

It did seem that Ireland had emerged successfully from the forced isolation of the war years to take her place as a Nation again in Europe. Initials like O.E.C.D., N.A.T.O. the E.E.C., E.U.R.A.T.O.M. were becoming a part of Irish economic jargon. There were more people holidaying abroad and frantically learning a European language. In contrast to London, though, it seemed to us that discussion in the Republic at any rate, was muted or even non-existent on certain matters like sex and religion. The Irish Catholic Church had not been a conscious agency of censorship regarding the second subject religion, but it had ensured by the very diligence of its mission, that the great majority of the people accepted their conservative Catholicism as the normal central value of Irish life. Catholicism itself and all that went with it seemed to be above discussion, whereas in London, one was always hearing the most outrageous opinions about every subject under the sun.

But there was hope of a change. Pope John had come along in 1958 with his questing crusading spirit. In spite of the conservative Irish Catholic Bishops, he had set people talking all over the world, in the saloon bars, the pubs, the cafes, the factories. It took more time in Ireland, but before he died in 1963, Pope John's presence has been truly felt through the first Vatican Council. The statement by the Archbishop of Dublin, Dr. McQuaid when he returned from the Council that nothing had changed, was greeted with derision by most people.

Ireland was changing. Truths learned at Mother's knee and at school had begun for many people, to take on a new meaning. Religion was no longer for many a subject for discussion in dark side chapels or confessional boxes, but a philosophy that should influence people's lives.

It was a time for questioning: How? Why? When? This was why the year 1963 in fact, was a great time to come back to Ireland as news editor of the Irish Times. It was a time for extending the frontiers, and the advent of Radio Telefis Eireann was an important milestone in this development. People were looking for new answers. Even children were not put off by their parents' impatience. Young people were kicking over the traces, and frustrated about the inanities of their own lives. They were not satisfied with the old society in Ireland with its easy acceptance of poverty and injustice as part of the will of God.

The role of the *Irish Times* in the circumstances was clear. It should be a forum for discussion, a mouthpiece for all minorities as well as the majority, and a paper with a clear-cut radical viewpoint. Guided by a radical editor this was the path we took, and I hope that the paper has played some little part therefore, in the opening up and development of Irish life in the past dozen years.

To achieve our objectives reporters were appointed in specialized fields, education, diplomacy, religion, the E.E.C., agriculture. The whole spectrum of Irish life was fully covered by specialist writers and opinionated contributors like Claud Cockburn, Liam de Paor, Benedict Kiely and Michael Viney.

The importance of women in Irish journalism, long before the Women's Liberation Movement began in Ireland was recognized in the Irish Times. The Women's Page 'Women First' became a forum for discussion of social, political and philosophical questions. Womens reporters were appointed on an equality basis with men and at one period their numbers were exactly half and half. The paper carried reports from every part of Ireland and as a result was able to lose its image as a purely Dublin paper. Long before the troubles began in Northern Ireland the *Irish Times* was giving full coverage to Stormont. The Irish language was a particular care. Three regular weekly columnists were hired, Sean O'Riordain, Brendan hEithir and Donal MacAmhliagh, and we gave a weekly half page to current affairs in Irish which I edited.

No cows were sacred and reporters and writers were given their heads to express the most unorthodox views. There was room too, of course, for the traditional and conservative values from contributors and letter writers. It is worth recording that when serious papers everywhere were declining and our competitors loosing readers the *Irish Times* went from 31,000 to 69,000. Readers will forgive the blowing of trumpets in the last few paragraphs but it is a necessary part of the story which I have tried to tell in these pages.

EPILOGUE

Earlier in this book (Chapter 4) I described the annual family journey by lorry to the Ring Gaeltacht. It was a kind of annual pilgrimage and holiday for the Foley family. To try and recapture some of the joy of that journey and to record the changes that have taken place I took a similar journey recently by car from Ferrybank to Ring.

I must report that the nostalgic world of Ring is no longer with us. The Irish language though it still lingers in that lovely area is only spoken intermittently, and it is no longer the main base of communication. The clusters of thatched houses which I recall from my childhood have long since made way for healthier, well built Gaeltacht cottages and the T.V. masts adorn most chimneys. The poverty, grinding and depriving as it was has largely gone, and young families are growing up in Ring full of confidence. Gone too are the little masted sailing boats to make way for bigger, less picturesque but more efficient fishing trawlers provided by Government aid.

Waterford Glass in its close-by Dungarvan Factory now employs about a dozen young men from the Ring area in highly paid permanent jobs. There is also a factory in what used to be Charlie Skuce's field opposite Mageen's bulging guest house where hundreds of people learned their Irish over the years. Mageen is dead and the guest house where so many people were well fed and housed for so little is now all silent, even during high summer.

It is fine to be able to report the prosperity of the Ring Peninsula, but sad to record the decline and loss of one of the richest Irish language areas in Ireland through lack of economic aid. It could have been so different if the factories and the financial injections had been applied at the right time before the people went to Birmingham, London, Yonkers and Brooklyn. Perhaps there is still time to rebuild the Ring Gaeltacht so that the work of all writers and great people of the district will forever be remembered in the way in which they cherished most – the Irish language spoken in Ballinagoul, Helvick, Bother na Sop and Shanakill.

Opposite the old Schoolhouse where the wind howled specially on winters' nights for us children is now the attractively designed public housing suburb of Rockingham. Similarly, the gardens of the Protestant Bishop which we used to raid for flowers for the annual procession is now a housing estate also. The lower slip where the tightly knit community of dockers lived has been demolished to make way for modern harbour developments. The "Mash" and Patsy Sutton's Bank on the River Suir, both essential parts of the Ferrybank village, have made way for dockland amenities, notably Bell Ferry which has linked Waterford with the Common Market. The old ferry service across the river which played such a major role in our education has gone too. Progress has captured all. Ferrybank is now an industrial complex.

Sad to see too as we drove towards the bridge that the Waterford red brick station with its unique clock that dominated the cobble stoned space for cars and animals has been destroyed and replaced by a C.I.E. utility building of no distinction. The older building had a reassuring dignity in its red façade, and one felt on returning to Waterford that one was really home when the station and its clock were there to welcome you.

The great expansive Waterford Quay is, as of yore, still

swept by cold east winds but now happily also alive with ships in the dock. Indeed, the city is fast recovering its title, "Waterford of the shippes" a common market bonus, perhaps. Reginald's Tower still stands sentinel-like and solid at the corner of the Quay and the Mall, as a reminder of the tortured history of this ancient Danish Fortress City. As we look over the river Suir, we notice that Fleming's Castle on Mount Misery is now the Ardree Hotel, an establishment which must enjoy one of the finest views of the largely unspoiled city and the lovely harbour of Waterford.

The best part of old Waterford, Blackfriars with its ruined church and old beauty and the Mall are still intact. The Protestant Bishop's residence (now offices) still remains, so does the Town Hall which houses the Theatre Royal and one of the best little theatres outside Dublin. It was here as a child that I saw all the great companies, Anew McMaster, Longford, Louis D'Alton and Edwards and MacLiammoir.

Parnell Street is as always solid and respectable, haven of doctors. But the old country car stand now has a supermarket and signs of much activity. Even more so than when the apple market was at its height. Out through the Manor and the Cork Road to see the real changes. Waterford Glass, an elegant structure in its own grounds, employs one third of the working population of the city. In the playing fields surrounding it there are groups of men indulging themselves in one of Waterford's ancient crafts, the game of hurling. The houses, ribbon like, stretch out as far as Holy Cross, four miles from the city which used to be in splendid isolation, and the center of much community life. Then we passed the little villages, the Sweep, Ballyduff, Kilmeaden, past Kilmacthomas in through the

125

right in the fields, and then on the broad sweep of road to Dungarvan. There are changes, changes everywhere. The houses are trimmer and mostly new. There are often two motorcars in the haggard, picnic areas and lay-bys, unheard of amenities in the old days. Grattan Square in Dungarvan unmolested by the hands of the developers and because the traders have done a bit of painting the whole town has a faintly continental air about it. There is a regularity and security about the Square in Dungarvan which seems to make it the natural market town of its prosperous hinterland, on the edge of the Golden Vale.

Now we take the winding, corkscrew road by the rim of the ocean from Dungarvan to Ring. The journey has no longer the wondrous excitement of those annual pilgrimages, but it is still satisfying to note that much of it is as it always was. There are men sitting on horse and cart driving out from Dungarvan, a postman on a bicycle is just finishing his rounds and little boys with school bags are walking along the country road from school.

Siobhan's pub with its thick thatch nestling in the corner of Bothar na Sop has been replaced by a modern structure a few yards away. Our own childhood Aladdin's Cave, otherwise the Ring Co-op where you could buy a sack of flour, a hundred of coal, a pair of silk stockings, a bundle of postcards, a box of chocolates, or a suit of clothes is now a ruined shed. All that talk of becoming a Museum came to nothing. It is a kind of museum anyway, as it stands, ruined and desolate.

Down in Ballinagoul which was once the nearest thing to an Irish commune, there are no big black jerseyed men with red hands to greet us now as of old. Radio Eireann voices from a cottage window . . . the Angelus bell. There is a sound of footsteps crunching on the road from the pier, then a firm shake hands and a welcoming voice; "Tá fáilte romhaibh." We're home.